D0110146

LOVE
TACTICS

LOVE TACTICS

THOMAS W. McKNIGHT &
ROBERT H. PHILLIPS

AVERY PUBLISHING GROUP INC.

Garden City Park, New York

Cover design by Martin Hochberg and Rudy Shur
In-House Editor Jacqueline Balla
Typeset by Multifacit Graphics, Aberdeen, NJ

Library of Congress Cataloging-in-Publication Data

McKnight, Thomas W.
      Love tactics: how to win the one you want / by Thomas W. McKnight
   & Robert H. Phillips.
             p.   cm.
      Includes index.
      ISBN 0-89529-367-6 (pbk.) : $7.95
      1. Love.   2. Courtship--United States. I. Phillips, Robert H.,
   1948-   . II. Title.
   HQ801.M488   1987   87-31935
   646.7'7--dc19   CIP

Copyright ©1988 by Thomas W. McKnight and Robert H. Phillips

All rights reserved. No part of this publication may be reproduced,
stored in a retrieval system, or transmitted, in any form or by
any means, electronic, mechanical, photocopying, recording, or
otherwise, without the prior written permission of the copyright
owner.

Printed in the United States of America

10

Contents

About the authors

Thomas W. McKnight is a human relations expert and lecturer who writes and speaks on the subject of romantic love. The insights he shares are drawn from many of his own observations as a single in the dating world, as well as from the many experiences confided in him by other singles anxiously engaged in "the quest."

A graduate of Brigham Young University, he has been a social worker for the last eight years, and is a regular columnist for the National Singles Register. He currently resides in Las Vegas, Nevada.

Robert H. Phillips, Ph.D., is a practicing psychologist on Long Island, New York. He is the founder and director of the Center for Coping with Chronic Conditions, a multi-service organization offering private and group counseling to help individuals cope with a variety of situations.

The author of three books on coping as well as numerous articles on a number of different subjects in psychology, Dr. Phillips has lectured at conventions, universities, and professional meetings throughout the country, and has appeared on local and national radio and television programs.

Acknowledgments

To Charles and Alois McKnight, whose commitment and love for one another has shown the way; to Rudy Shur, without whose confidence this message of hope might never have been so widely shared; and most of all, to God, who is the true and ultimate source of all love.

T.W.M.

This book is dedicated to all those wonderful people—family and friends—who have always been there for me, providing love and support when I needed it, and sharing progress and growth together.

I must acknowledge the participation of Sharon Balaban and Jacqueline Balla for their patience and expertise in processing, editing, and preparing this project.

R.H.P.

Preface

Whether this book ever becomes a best seller remains to be seen, but it really ought to be! Why? The answer is painfully obvious to anyone who has ever felt the agonizing frustration of not having their love reciprocated!

Isn't it ironic that, in spite of the many technological advances made within the last century, people today are still as frustrated as ever in their quest for true love? Our society is full of individuals who have disappointedly abandoned their idealistic dreams of romantic fulfillment. It almost seems a law of nature that the one *you* want never wants you back, while the ones who *are* interested in you are simply incapable of stirring your emotions! Love forever looms on the horizon, but is just out of reach.

Many have given up, deciding that nothing can be done to alter an apparently loveless destiny. They have resigned themselves to going through life, taunted by the prospects of love, but never truly possessing it. You may have experienced such feelings of helplessness yourself! If so, then this book is the answer to your prayers.

Love Tactics demonstrates why there is a very real reason not to give up hope. Love is *not* the mere result of chance meetings determined by pure luck. Believe it or not, love is a *predictable human response!* It results whenever a person's key psychological needs are satisfied. It's true that, on occasion, love does seem to occur accidentally. But even in these cases, such relationships still conform to the principles of romantic behavior outlined in this book! Anyone who chooses to consciously apply these rules of love in an intelligent manner need not go through life unloved! Succeeding in romance, then, only requires becoming aware of your ability to modify and influence the emotional moods, attitudes, and behaviors of others through well-proven psychological techniques. We're not talking about taking unfair advantages—just using strategic common sense!

As you can probably imagine, it would be impossible to include all the different strategies, techniques, and tips that can possibly be used in winning the one you want. Rather, *Love Tactics* provides the basic formula from which you will be able to derive your own solution to your particular circumstances. As you read the book, you'll find yourself becoming more enthusiastic, confident, and eager to approach others in an effort to win the person of your dreams.

Of the many lessons you'll learn in *Love Tactics*, however, remember this important truth above all else: *The way to true love is not to sit back and wait for the person of your dreams to magically appear. Rather, it involves choosing the one you want above all others, and then winning them over using known principles of human romantic behavior.*

Yes, you *can* win the one you want! You don't have to settle for anything (or anyone) less! The dream is in sight! It's merely a matter of psychology. *Love Tactics* will acquaint you with the science of human behavior as it relates to love and romance, and teach you how to *win the one you want!*

1

An Introduction: General Strategy

The general strategy behind *Love Tactics* is quite simple. It is based on the premise that romantic love has three essential parts: 1. *Friendship* 2. *Respect* and 3. *Passion*. Because love will fail if it lacks one or more of these necessary ingredients, the only way you can be successful in winning the one you want is by learning how to cultivate *all three feelings* in their heart for you.

THE HOUSE OF LOVE

We can compare a love relationship to a housing unit. As long as it is complete and functions the way it should, it makes a pleasant abode. There is no incentive to move out, since all one's needs for shelter and comfort are being adequately met.

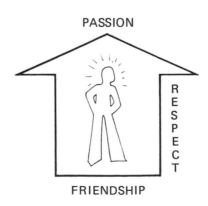

But what if the resident came home, night after night, only to discover that there was no roof? Or floor? Or walls? It wouldn't be long before they would be looking for a new home!

Sometimes, out of desperation, a person may jump prematurely into a situation that meets some of their more immediate needs. But if this situation doesn't satisfy their other emotional requirements as well, they will eventually realize their mistake (and move out)!

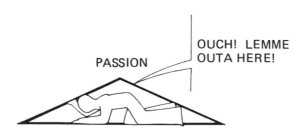

AN EMPTY HOUSE

Why does love sometimes fail? In most cases it can be traced to the absence of one or more of these three essential elements. Together, these elements contain all the ingredients necessary for the development of romantic fulfillment. Just as a house would be incomplete without a roof, walls, or foundation, so would a relationship be unfulfilling without friendship, respect, and passion. If just one of these components fails to germinate and develop, then the person lacking these feelings for the other cannot help but feel a little dissatisfied (yes, even cheated!). The relationship would be about as rewarding as sitting down on a three-legged stool and finding out (too late) that it only has two legs!

The basic strategy, then, to win *and* keep the one you want is to cultivate *friendship*, *respect*, and *passion* in your relationship with that person. *Only* when all three of these essential elements are present can you hope to enjoy love at its very best!

FRIENDSHIP

Before you can truly win someone's heart, you must first become friends with that person. Although this may appear easy, it really is not. True friendship meets a person's deep, emotional needs. A wise person once defined *a friend* as "someone you can think out loud in front of." In light of this definition, then, we might all find ourselves reevaluating who we really consider to be our true friends!

To become a true friend, you must learn to meet that person's basic human emotional needs. These include:

1. *Attention.* You'll need to show the other person that you are consciously aware of his or her existence.

2. *Understanding.* Just communicating your awareness that the person exists isn't enough. You also need to show that you're aware of how *they feel* about—and perceive—the world around them.

3. *Acceptance.* This means showing the person that you still value being with them, even though at times their behavior or attitudes may be less than praiseworthy.

4. *Appreciation.* You can satisfy this need by recognizing those redeeming qualities that the other person possesses.

5. *Affection.* This is easily shown by reassuring the person that, regardless of comparisons with others, he or she is still very special to you and, therefore, very important. Sometimes this can be communicated by no more than a *simple touch.*

As you begin to meet a person's five basic emotional friendship needs, you'll be helping that person along the road to greater happiness. In return, he or she will develop a subconscious emotional dependence on you. This dependence is an essential part of any romantic relationship. In order to encourage them to voluntarily place this trust in you, however, you must first prove worthy of their trust.

Behavior Principle #1:
People Subconsciously Grow Dependent Upon
Those Who Satisfy Their Emotional Needs

The first objective of *Love Tactics* is to show you how to satisfy the emotional friendship needs of the one you want—and to do it better and more completely than anyone they have ever met before! The various techniques described in this book will help you to easily accomplish this.

RESPECT

While it is true that pure *friendship* is the engine of romantic love, *respect* is the gas that makes it go! People are motivated to be with, and to associate themselves with, those persons whom they truly respect.

How do we come to respect someone? Respect is an acquired attitude. For the most part, it is usually based on our perception of a person's independence and self-reliance. The more capable a person seems to be of getting along in life without having to rely on us, the more likely we are to actually feel drawn towards that person. The opposite also holds true. The more easily a person becomes dependent upon us, the more "turned off" we become. When people act possessive towards us and show an inclination to "cling," our degree of respect for them declines. It is quite normal to feel a need to escape from such persons.

Behavior Principle #2:
People Are Most Attracted To Those Who Exhibit Some Degree Of Aloofness and Self-Reliant Independence

So if we want to win someone's heart fully and completely, we must be perceived (by that person) as being capable of surviving quite well without him or her. At the same time, however, we cannot neglect their very real psychological need for friendship. This presents us with the task of performing a delicate balancing act. Again, *Love Tactics* will show you how to accomplish both objectives!

PASSION

The crowning experience of romantic love is the ultimate sensation we know as *passion*. We can only enjoy something in life to the degree that we truly long for it. Therefore, levels of romantic desire must be raised to a fever pitch if the romantic experience is really going to satisfy our need for a fulfilling relationship and become the ecstasy we always dreamed of. This brings us to one of the most widely-known principles of human behavior.

Behavior Principle #3:
People Want What They Can't Have!

What happens when people become overly confident that a desirable object is "theirs for the taking?" They'll almost always take such a treasure for granted. (Frequently, they'll even abuse it!) Therefore, if you want to successfully build a romantic relationship with someone, it is imperative that you not ignore this principle. Otherwise, you will wind up forfeiting the rewards that you would ultimately have reaped!

By using the tactics discussed in the remainder of this book, you can build a romantic fire in someone else's heart that will blaze exclusively for *you*. Once begun, this fire will burn so brightly that the remaining embers will continue to glow for a lifetime! So there is no time like the present to concentrate on fueling that fire with the appropriate elements.

The secret to building passion in another person can be expressed in the form of a mathematical equation:

$$HOPE + DOUBT = PASSION$$

COMMITMENT

Falling in love is ultimately a rational, conscious act. It's a willful decision to let down our last remaining emotional barriers and become wholly vulnerable to another human being. But even though this final decision is a conscious and rational act, it is actually based upon emotional feeling, despite the natural tendency to deny this. As J. Pierpont Morgan reportedly once quipped, "Every man has two reasons for doing, or not doing, a thing: One that sounds good, and a real one."

Behavior Principle #4:
People Make Conscious Decisions Based On Subconscious Feelings, Then Justify Their Decisions With Reasons That Sound Good

It doesn't matter how logical it seems that a particular person should be in love with you. If the proper emotional attitudes have not been cultivated inside that person, then a meaningful commitment to you in a relationship simply will not occur. It is true that a person may commit himself to you based on sheer will power alone, but that person would always feel a void and emptiness inside. This would undermine the strength of anyone's commitment to you in the long run, no matter how sincere it might be at first.

On the other hand, if the proper feelings of friendship, respect, and passion have been appropriately cultivated in the relationship, it would be practically impossible for the person to resist making such a commitment to you, regardless of other "logical" reasons why it shouldn't happen.

If it's your desire to truly be loved by the one you want—if you want a complete, fulfilling, and totally reciprocated commitment from the person of your dreams—then get smart! Use the understanding of human behavior you will acquire from this book to your advantage! Cultivate friendship, respect, and passion in your relationship, and you will see how commitment to you will follow as naturally as day follows night!

Simply put, the general strategy of this book is based on the philosophy, *"love begets love."* The key is to communicate that love. It begins with your commitment to love another human being. It results in that person's commitment to love you back.

2

Acting With Self-Assurance

---

*Principle: People are most readily drawn to you
when you radiate a positive self-image!*

Now you're ready to begin! You're willing to give it a try and
go after the one you want! You're hopeful that this book will
finally unravel the mystery of how to do it! But deep down
you're still wondering if you've got what it takes. You have
self-doubts. You're afraid.

Let those fears be dispelled! True enough, *you* are where
this whole process begins. But *we* have faith in you! We know
from our own personal experience that you (whoever you are)
have within you capacities for greatness yet untapped! We
haven't the slightest doubt that you, in fact, are *already* great—
however hidden from view this side of you may have been
until now.

This chapter contains a number of tactics that will help you
to feel more confident about yourself. As this confidence
grows, you will become more emotionally prepared to successfully win the one you want. Additionally, you will radiate

more charm to help enchant and draw the one you want *to you.*

Whitney Houston sings that "learning to love yourself is the greatest love of all . . . " It is understandable that, unless a person feels good about himself, then he will not be able to show much love to another person. Therefore, it's important for you to learn to *like yourself* as much as possible. Our whole focus here can be summed up in the words *positive self-image.*

VIBES

Have you ever noticed that people tend to pick up vibes from others they are with? Think about the people you enjoy being with the most. You undoubtedly pick up positive vibes from these people, and that's why you enjoy being with them. So it makes sense for you to try to radiate these same types of positive vibes to others. But how is this done? Again, *by feeling better about yourself.* A positive self-image gives off positive vibes. This will be apparent in your face, your speech, and your behavior in general.

The vibes you give off will become an "aura" that brightens the atmosphere around you, engulfing and captivating those individuals with whom you come in contact. Others will enjoy being with you because of your positive attitude. This is the true source of that personal magnetism we know of as *charisma.*

LOVE TACTIC #1 Be Nice To Number One (Yourself)!

Before you can begin to glow with increased self-confidence, you must practice treating yourself with kindness, tolerance, and mercy! Research has indicated that many people are harder on themselves than they need be. They are too negative and self-critical in their private thoughts. Constantly bad-mouthing yourself will only serve to keep your self-image low. And, consequently, such self-deprecation can also diminish a person's ability to win the one they want.

So cut it out! As a first step toward winning the one you want, commit yourself here and now to break any such patterns of self-abuse. Make up your mind to no longer put yourself down. From now on, it is essential that you *go easier on yourself and be nice to Number One (yes, that's you!)* True, you may not be perfect, but it is vital to the overall plan that you at least treat yourself with respect.

How do you begin, if such self put-downs are already a habit with you? First, become consciously aware of exactly how much you do this. Take note of when you say something negative to yourself. Mentally keep track of your personal thoughts and self-dialogues. What did you say? What were your reasons for being upset with yourself?

Even if you get angry at something you've done, realize that you can learn from your mistakes. You *can* change. Criticize your *behavior* instead of blaming *yourself*. Emphasize the action rather than the person. How much better it is to say, "I did a dumb thing" than "I'm dumb!" Turn those negatives around! You can always find something positive in yourself.

Sure, this requires letting yourself off the hook sometimes when you blow it. But who doesn't deserve a good dose of mercy from time to time? And we promise that the improvement you will see in yourself because of this will surpass any results you hope to achieve by self-chastisement! In this way, you'll gradually improve the way you feel about yourself. As you feel more confident, it will begin to show and the people around you will respond to the aura that you radiate.

This is not to say that you should engage in the practice of excusing your faults, or bragging to others. Just realize that everyone has faults. Making mistakes does not make you a "bad" person. In fact, being human can actually work in your favor. As one young single person explained, "I don't want someone who is *too* perfect!"

Second, realize that nobody is perfect. Everyone (absolutely *everyone*) makes mistakes and, heck, you are certainly entitled to your share of them! Mistakes do not make a person inferior—only human!

Third, don't become discouraged if you're having a hard time shaking your feelings of inferiority, even after what we've just told you in the paragraph above! Be aware that if you are plagued with a bit of an inferiority complex, you are not alone. In fact, *most* people in the world secretly feel inferior to others, though they obviously don't go around broadcasting this. So your feelings of inadequacy are *not* the end of the world. You can *still* win the one you want, in spite of this. Millions of others have! But the more accepting you are of yourself, *without putting yourself down,* the greater an advantage you will have.

Fourth, realize that no matter what frailties you may have exhibited in the past, if you are capable of *recognizing* them as faults then you possess the capacity to improve yourself. This is a very important point.

Last, control your inner thinking. Indulging in negative thoughts can be one of the most destructive things you do. How do you know you're thinking negatively? By your feelings! Whenever you're feeling depressed, angry, guilty, lonely, sad, hopeless, or another upsetting emotion, you can be sure you have negative thoughts on your mind. These may sometimes be subconscious, however. Get those feelings out in the open! Ask yourself, "What exactly am I feeling? Why am I feeling this way? What specific incidents are making me feel this way?" You can't stop feelings and impressions from popping into your head, but you can certainly control how you react to them! Practice the "red flag" approach. Identify negative thoughts as soon as they appear in your mind—in essence, "red flagging" them. As soon as you're aware that they exist, defuse them. Squarely face up to them, examine them, and analyze them for what they are. Be thorough. Be exhaustive. Take several days to do this, if necessary, and then *write those thoughts down!* Ask yourself which of those things can be changed. Ask yourself which ones cannot. Then attempt to change the ones that can be changed, and accept the ones that cannot. You may be depressed because you can't change everything in your life, but you'll be surprised at how much better you'll feel about your life just by changing the few things you *do* have control over. This will greatly increase your self-esteem and heighten your ability to win the one you want!

GIVE YOURSELF CREDIT

Of course, the *best* thing you can do to boost your self-esteem is to realize the many good things you *already* have going for you. What *are* your good qualities? What are the positive aspects of you, the person? Every person has some. Think about yours. Again, sit down with a pencil and paper and compile a list of your good qualities. At first, you might feel like you don't have any (or very few). That's not true. Every person has positive traits that they should be given credit for. You, too, should get your share. You'll be surprised how your list will continue to grow, once you get started!

Think about the positive things you're able to do, the positive things you've accomplished in your life. Identify the people who like you, the people who look up to and respect you. Write down those things that you actually *like* about yourself: *character traits, talents, achievements.* Write down the nice things you've done for others; any acts of kindness you can remember showing someone else. Write down the skills you possess naturally or have developed. You'll be surprised at the effect that this list will have on your self-esteem! You'll feel better about yourself than you have in a long time!

Even after you've completed this exercise and have moved on to other parts of this book, there's no reason not to continue adding to your list of positives as you become aware of them. Make this ongoing list a regular part of your life, which you tuck away in a drawer to review and revise from time to time. (This is one way Benjamin Franklin always kept his life improving!) In this way, even when you're feeling down or suffering from a shaky self-image, you can review this list. It can help you to feel better about yourself. Remember: *Identifying your positive characteristics, as well as thinking more positively, are two of the most important ways you can help to improve your self-image.* And as your acceptance of yourself manifests itself to others, they, too, will follow your lead and become more accepting of you.

LOVE TACTIC #2 Identify Your Goals

Something very strange happens when you start to center your life—and happiness—around another person. It gets out of kilter. It gets out of whack. Oddly enough, even though there is no greater joy than that of being loved by another person, as soon as the gratification of that particular need becomes the primary focus of our life's existence it will elude us. It is paradoxical, but true, that in order to successfully win someone's love and devotion, you must first learn how to be happy *without their love and devotion*—at least to some degree. Happy relationships seldom result from joining two unhappy people together. Happy relationships arise from the union of *two happy individuals!* What this means is that your best chances for possessing the love you've always dreamed of come from pursuing your own individual destiny and attempting to find as much personal satisfaction and happiness as you can on your own—alone. As you do this, love will follow *you*. In this regard, love is like a shadow. It runs from you when chased directly, but when you give up on it and turn to walk away, it will always be found tagging along behind you!

Not long ago, one of the authors prodded a friend about when he and his girlfriend were going to get around to "tying the knot." The friend suddenly became very sober and frankly admitted that something was lacking in his attitude towards her. "She's a great girl," he said, "but it's like she has no goals in life other than to get married. I think I need somebody more goal-oriented than that!"

Whether you realize it or not, most of us subconsciously want someone who is goal-oriented and heading someplace—

even without us! You, too, must establish a course of direction if you hope to attract the one you want.

To pursue your own destiny, though, requires identifying your own set of personal goals and planning ways of achieving them. Having a plan of action—having goals and anticipating the particular steps necessary to achieve each goal—is one of the most essential processes for happy and successful living.

Goal-setting can be a very positive experience. It focuses on your positive potential, rather than your negative deficiencies. This, in itself, will reassure you of your true limitless value and help you to convey greater self-confidence to others. Have you ever been concerned that the one you want might not desire you because you lack certain qualities? Then among the goals you can establish for yourself are ways to improve in these areas! Your self-confidence will be further increased as you have the experience of feeling yourself actually improve, as you acquire some of the qualities and characteristics that you so admire in others!

But perhaps the greatest benefit of identifying goals and planning ways to achieve them is the sense of power that comes from actively taking steps to assume control of your own life! Think about the times when you've felt good about your own life and compare them to the times when you haven't. You'll realize that, in most cases, you were feeling good when you were actively taking steps to achieve something in your life. On the other hand, when you sat around doing nothing, being bored, or hoping for something to happen, you probably felt much less positive about yourself. Without definite goals to work towards, you'll stagnate and lose confidence in yourself, floundering aimlessly. (Just what you need to impress the one you want, right?) Goals help you to determine the exact direction you want to move in, so you can proceed with confidence!

Picture the following scenario: Your car is filled with gas. You start the ignition, shift into gear, and pull out of your parking space. All of a sudden you realize, "I don't know where I'm going!"

Sound strange? Yet how many of us are content to do this day after day with a vehicle so much more precious than any car—our very lives!! Don't you fall into this trap! *Love Tactics* demands that you take a more active role in the management of your own life! By identifying personal goals and taking steps to achieve them, your love life will fall into place naturally. Indeed, it may surprise you how naturally!!

1. Decide what you want. Think about your present wishes and desires. Dream big, but break your dream down into small enough steps so that you always have something to do next. Ask yourself, "What exactly do I want to accomplish in the near future? What do I want to achieve?" Make sure your goals consist of things that you, personally, can work towards. Don't depend on the whims of others to help you achieve your goals. Remember, you can't depend on somebody else to accomplish your goals for you. You're the only one you can count on to implement your plan!

2. Write down your goals. For some reason goals become real the moment they are written down. You then have a record of what you've decided to shoot for, which will help you to keep track of your progress. Otherwise, it's far too easy to forget your goals and not follow through.

3. Know your priorities. Of the many things you would like to accomplish, decide which ones are the most important. Determine which goal you want to work towards first.

4. Attach a time frame. The difference between a goal and a wish is that a goal has a definite time frame attached to it, within which we intend to do certain things to help accomplish that goal.

5. Break down your goals into daily tasks. When we talk about setting goals, we're not just talking about life-long ones. We're also talking about goals for your day-to-day

existence. What good would any business person be if he or she didn't know what had to be accomplished at work each day? How effective could a teacher be if he only thought about the semester exam and neglected planning the daily lessons? You will be most effective by breaking down your long-term goals into daily sub-goals.

Deciding on a specific plan of action—forming goals and planning the steps necessary to achieve each one—is one of the most essential processes for happy and successful living. Do it! As you will eventually discover, it will assist you in winning the one you want!

LOVE TACTIC #3 Relax!

Anyone who has ever had a really serious crush on someone is aware of the tension and anxiety associated with even being in the same room with that person! You think you're just about going to die, right? Your legs feel like putty, and you're afraid to speak because you're sure you'll only be able to manage a hoarse whisper (with a couple of squeaks thrown in for good measure!). Your instincts tell you to hide this nervousness, while your good sense tells you you can't—which only heightens the tension you are feeling! What's a self-respecting person supposed to do in a situation like this? Why, *relax*, of course!

Up until now, however, nobody's really been able to tell you how to accomplish that feat, have they? Today, though, you are going to learn something that will be more helpful to you than all the relaxation exercises in the world. Are you ready? Here it is: *It's o.k. to be nervous!* Did you get that? Let's go over it one more time, because it's a hard concept to grasp: *It's o.k. to be nervous!* That's right! The very thing we go around trying to avoid all our lives is not so terrible after all!

The real problem isn't our nervousness, but our unwillingness to forge ahead with our plans as long as we think it shows! Actually, the power to succeed is in us all along, but we are deceived into not using it. So relax! Realize that it's o.k. to be nervous! You'd be surprised to learn how many people will actually be *more* attracted to you when they sense your courage to act in spite of your fears. A shaky voice is music to their ears and a greater compliment than you can imagine! This doesn't mean you have to discuss your feelings of nervousness. Just be willing to go with the flow. Don't go to any unnatural extremes one way or the other, to either suppress your nervousness or to enhance it.

You might as well enjoy it while you can, in fact, because it won't last. Once you start acting in spite of your fears, they will soon begin to dissipate. Would you like to know the most effective cure for nervousness? It's *experience!*

Now why might it be important to learn to relax as part of your quest for the one you want? Well, you obviously want to feel that you're making the best possible impression, right? You want to come across as a confident person, don't you? Well, being able to relax can be a very important tool to help you feel like you're in control of the situation. By finding an inner calm and peace in your quiet, reflective moments alone, you'll realize that your entire world doesn't depend on a single encounter with another person. You'll find inner resources of self-confidence that you can fall back on whenever your anxiety level would otherwise be reaching the "red zone."

There's another reason, too, why it's good to be relaxed when you're with others. When you convey a cool, calm demeanor, it helps others to follow your lead and feel calm and relaxed *with you!* On the other hand, if you place too much importance on every rendezvous with another person, and convey nervous desperation continuously, it will produce uneasiness in the person you're with and may cause them to be a little more "on guard" and defensive.

The more carefree and relaxed you are, the more free your subconscious mind will be to guide your actions in social settings. And, like an automatic homing device, you'll find that trusting your intuitive powers will lead you where you want to go.

Of course we perform best when we are free of anxiety and relaxed. But how, you ask, can you possibly keep from freezing up in the most important situation of your entire life? The answer: You can't! So don't feel so overly distraught when you do! The compensation for all this is that once you really blow a situation badly, you'll feel amazingly more confident in similar encounters in the future. So don't ever be afraid of blowing a situation. There will always be a benefit to you, either way, no matter what the outcome. You always win, either by accidentally coming off just like you wanted, or by gaining experience that will make you ever so much more suave and cool in future encounters. So, relax! You just can't lose!

LOVE TACTIC #4 Talk With Confidence

Wouldn't you like to be able to talk to the one you want with confidence? Then it's important that you be accepting of yourself. Don't inhibit your efforts to converse with him or her because of your fears of what they might think of you. *What you say is not nearly as important as the fact that you say something.* As you become accustomed to not letting your fears prevent you from speaking, your ability to make more sense and to be more entertaining will improve.

STARTING A CONVERSATION

What is the best way to start a conversation with someone new? People are more uncomfortable with this aspect of social interaction than any other. There is not only pressure on the person trying to initiate the conversation, but also on the person being approached. The person being approached may be put "on the spot" because he or she is concerned that their response will appear inadequate or foolish. However, a few key techniques can put everyone at ease. Starting a conversation need not be that difficult. In fact, once you get over your initial reluctance, you'll find making conversation an effective instrument to help you win the one you want.

You must first realize that conversation involves more than words. It also includes eye contact and, to a lesser extent, body language. Realize, too, that facial expressions are a crucial part of the conversation process. If you continue smiling even as you stumble over your words, you can be assured that you'll make a good impression.

CONVERSATION ANXIETIES

Now let's get down to basics. One of the main reasons why you might feel uncomfortable starting a conversation with someone new is the fear of rejection. You may fear that if you don't come across in just the right way you'll be rejected. How humiliating! How shameful! You can just picture yourself slinking off in embarrassment. Let such thoughts be dispelled, though! The key to successful conversation isn't the use of fancy words in an attempt to make a good impression. The secret is to come across as a warm, caring person! And as long as you are making a sincere effort to communicate by putting yourself on the line for someone, that's exactly how you'll come across! If you're sincere, you'll never make a bad impression. It's when we try to be *impressive* that we get ourselves into trouble.

WHAT TO SAY

Is there anything you can say to get the ball rolling? Yes, just about *anything!* For lack of something better, even old hackneyed phrases that indicate you've been watching old movies will do! You might feel funny walking up to somebody you've never met and saying something like, "Excuse me, but haven't I seen you somewhere before?," but such efforts work! It's part of human nature to be flattered by such attention, and the people you approach in this fashion will eat it up!

SMALL TALK

Making small talk is the usual way to break the ice and meet new people. This is because such talk focuses on non-threatening, non-personal subjects such as the weather, surrounding location, or other people. The advantage of small talk is that it gives a person a chance to warm up to you a bit and learn to trust you *before* making themselves vulnerable to you. A gentle, slow approach is better than coming on like a gangbuster! However, small talk alone won't get you very far in developing a deep relationship! It merely serves as a temporary transition to more meaningful conversation.

"BIGGER" TALK

As soon as it's appropriate, you need to personalize the conversation. You need to discuss feelings and attitudes that are normally missing in small talk. Once small talk has gotten the ball rolling, gradually direct the conversation towards the other person. Ask questions that show an interest in their opinions. Ask about their experiences. Mention something about yourself occasionally, but do so only as it relates to the other person (to show you can identify with what they are saying). Quickly turn the spotlight back on them. If the other person asks you some sincere questions about yourself, answer them without getting carried away. Remember that their interest has its limits! In the early stages, especially, you only want to reveal enough about yourself to whet their appetite and make them want to know more! Always maintain some mystery about yourself. This will keep them coming back around. Think of your conversations as a great banquet, in which *they* are the main course and you are the seasoning. You don't want the main course to be *too* spicy!

Of course, we hardly need mention here that you must avoid even the *appearance* of bragging. Nothing is as repulsive as the person who seems to get "high" on recounting endless facts about himself. Another no-no involves speaking negatively of others. Unfortunately, some people like to make conversation by putting other people down in some way. Uniting themselves with anyone who will join them in such backstabbing ventures gives them a false sense of acceptance. But don't you fall into this trap! All it does is sow seeds of distrust in everyone you meet. If you would put down someone else, how can they be sure you won't do the same thing to them? So avoid this as well as other forms of negative gossip! It will leave a bad impression on the one you want. It's better to speak positively and supportingly of others. As the saying goes, "If you can't say somethin' nice, don't say nothin' at all!"

In conclusion, then, realize that you must accept the responsibility for initiating and maintaining successful conversation if you hope to win the one you want. You can't leave such a vital element of a developing relationship to chance. *You must be in control.* This doesn't mean you should be doing most of the talking. *You keep control largely by listening and asking questions.* Invite the other person to do most of the talking, but make sure that you have plenty of fuel available to feed the fire when the flame looks like it's dying out! A little pre-planning can help out here. Have some ideas ahead of time regarding topics you can *ask them about.* (Many years ago, one of the authors of this book was quite nervous about an upcoming date and how he could keep the conversation flowing comfortably. He finally resorted to writing down a list of possible topics on a 3" x 5" index card and secretly referring to it throughout the evening. It worked great!) But don't get hung up on the particulars. Just remember to be warm and caring. Even if you're not totally confident of your conversational abilities, you can show that you care by being a good listener. Others like that! Remember—people don't care how much you *know* until they know how much you *care!*

LOVE TACTIC #5   Know What You Want (In A Prospective Mate)!

Before going on to the rest of the love tactics in this book, you'll need to have a clear idea of what characteristics and qualities you're looking for in the one you want. At times, the going will get quite tough, and being sure that the one you want is the one you *really* want will be the only source of strength and motivation you'll have to fall back on. When your goal is more defined, you'll be more committed to following through and doing what is necessary to win them over.

Some people don't realize that they are attracted by certain qualities. They've never really analyzed their *reasons* for becoming enamored in the first place. For them, love remains a mystery. They are like a ship in the midst of an ocean without a map to guide them, drifting to whatever isle fate happens to choose, and having no control whatsoever over their own destiny.

But you must be different! For those who understand the forces that guide them, and who know where they want to go, it is possible to chart their own course! And that's exactly what we expect *you* to do!

First, you should make a list of all the people you can remember having crushes on in your life. Then, next to each name, write down all the things you remember liking about that person. What exactly attracted you to them? Was it their smile? Their eyes? The way they laughed? Think of the kind of person they were. Were they kind? Self-assured? Intelligent? Did they have a good sense of humor? These are the kinds of things you'll want to ask yourself. Then review this list and ask yourself what other qualities you would like the person of your dreams to have. This will take a lot of careful thought. Soon you should come up with a pretty good profile of your ideal person. Now don't panic just because you don't think such a person exists! This is just a starting point.

Knowing what characteristics you'd like in a person will better prepare you to begin your search. This doesn't mean, however, that your expectations will remain inflexible. You'll be surprised at how easy it will be to adjust your wants according to the real live prospects available. Your list is just a frame of reference for starting out. Obviously, you may revise your list if you like, and you will discover that you are still attracted to many people who don't meet up to all your initial, ideal expectations. But knowing what that ideal is will give you power in your search!

LOVE TACTIC #6 Plan Out Where To Hunt

As much help as *Love Tactics* can be when you have actually found someone you want, it wouldn't be complete without some suggestions as to *where* you may find a prospective mate. This section will briefly discuss a few settings where you might plant a few romantic seeds.

ON THE JOB

This may be one of your very best sources of meeting people, for a couple of reasons. First, you spend a lot of time there and can become intimately acquainted with customers, clients, and co-workers. Second, because your activities are focused around other business, it can take some of the pressure off male/female relationships.

Countless couples have met through work-related circumstances! Although some people feel it is risky to become romantically involved with someone you associate with at work, others state that it is worth the risk! Only you can decide if the gamble is worth it in your particular situation.

SPECIAL INTEREST GROUPS

Another gold mine for potential romance lies in special hobby groups. A photography club, skiing club, health club, etc. probably exists not far from your home. You might obtain a catalogue from an adult education program, or a community college with continuing education courses, and browse through topics of interest. This will give you an idea of the types of clubs and organizations that may already exist in your community. And, if not, you can always take a class! A classroom is probably *the* best place to become acquainted with members of the opposite sex!

Service organizations, too, provide a fertile field for seeds of introduction to grow and flourish. When you work side by side with someone for a charitable cause, it makes relationship development as easy as 1-2-3.

While you're at it, don't discount the possibility of going to your place of worship! People you meet here are often more sincere about seeking a permanent and lasting relationship than those you might meet in other settings. One young man in the armed forces discovered that the best place to meet women was *in church!* It seemed that his most stable and enjoyable relationships began in such settings! (Additionally, the girls' parents would usually invite him over for Sunday dinner!)

Don't assume that you need special skills or must meet rigid requirements in order to get involved in any of the above-named groups or associations. A simple phone call asking for information and expressing an interest in getting involved is usually all it takes. Most people will be happy to help you out.

REFERRALS THROUGH FRIENDS

No matter how you decide to improve your social circulation, there is one method you must not miss out on. Rely on your already existing network of friends! This is often one of the safest ways to proceed, even though you may not know ahead of time who you're going to be "fixed up" with. But because your friend is screening your date before you meet him or her, you can be assured that the person is relatively "safe!"

And you can be creative! One young man had a married couple he knew bring their single girlfriends to social or athletic events where, unknown to her, he occupied the fourth seat. Because none of them ever let on to the girl that he was part of their group, the "pressure" was off! It was easy for them to get to know each other.

THE SINGLES SCENE

The problem with bars is that they are largely associated with temporary alliances. Many people refuse to go to bars because they consider them "pickup joints" where the best you can hope for is a "one-night stand." Deep down we are really looking for a lasting, permanent relationship. Therefore, we don't want to have to settle for table scraps when we could be feasting at the banquet of true love.

Dances don't have such a negative reputation. But it may be difficult to meet someone at a dance because you first have to go up to a person you don't know and break the ice. On the other hand, once you overcome this fear, you may find this an especially effective (and enjoyable) way to spend your time.

Dating services and singles clubs can be another fruitful way of meeting people. However, it's usually a good idea to research these organizations before joining them to be sure they're reputable. Singles groups that are affiliated with religious organizations or community centers are usually good bets, but if there is a profit motive involved you have to be a little careful. Be more wary of small, privately-advertised organizations or services that don't have any known affiliations or where you don't know any members.

Personal ads in newspapers and magazines are becoming more and more commonplace. There was a time when this was considered a sleazy approach, but today respectable people from every profession and age group are trying them, often with a great deal of success. If you decide to use this method, make sure you put your ad in a reputable publication. Before placing an ad, review some of the other ads in the publication so you have an idea what to say. The largest and most reputable singles register we know of in the United States is the National Singles Register, published bi-weekly from Norwalk, California. There are numerous success stories of happily-married couples who met through their personal columns. Their address is P.O. Box 567, Norwalk, California, 90650. Write to them for further information.

A WORD (OR TWO) TO THE SHY

We are aware that some of you reading this book may have a very difficult time getting started because of super-shyness. This is nothing to be ashamed of! In fact, being super-shy is actually quite common in this country. Many, many people (more than you realize) are so afraid of encountering others that they keep themselves shut up at home constantly. We understand your dilemma. If you are having a hard time getting started, may we offer a few suggestions?

First, practice dealing with people over the telephone. Call the operator if you have to and try asking for phone numbers. From there, you can practice calling bookstores and asking them what books they have on a particular subject, or calling businesses listed in the yellow pages and asking about the services they offer and their prices. The more relaxed you become, the more creative you can become in the types of questions you ask.

When you feel you are ready to confront people face-to-face, you might try a grocery store, library, restaurant, or other public place. You might begin by asking employees for some help in finding a particular item, or what they have available. Eventually you can work your way up to asking other customers for the time or directions to another location.

Don't be embarrassed if you must resort to such seemingly simple steps to increase your self-confidence. Consider Demosthenes, the great Greek orator, who was initially very uncomfortable with public speaking. He used to practice by himself at the beach by putting pebbles in his mouth and trying to speak clearly above the sound of the waves breaking on the beach. With such persistence and desire you, too, can gain supreme self-confidence!

Eventually, you'll be ready for some dates. When you are, if it's still hard for you to approach someone directly, having a friend set you up on a blind date may be a good idea. Don't be afraid to use this option frequently. Why? The more practice you get, the more self-assured you'll become. If you're afraid you'll run out of things to say, write down possible topics and keep a list in your pocket, as was previously mentioned. If you can't remember what you had written down, excuse yourself for a moment and secretly review your list.

Remember, even shy people can win the one they want! You may have to take small steps in the beginning, but those small steps will help accomplish your goal as surely as the big ones, as long as you keep on practicing. "If at first you don't succeed, try, try, again!" Good luck and happy hunting!

3

Taking the Offensive

Principle: People are like mirrors, always reflecting the same attitudes that they think others have towards them.

The one you want is out there waiting for someone to love! The miracle is that *you can be that person!* All you have to do is take the initiative to act. It's already in the program for them to respond. Human beings have been designed in such a way as to return those feelings of love which they recognize as genuine. The challenge you have is to (1) Make sure your love *is* real and (2) Effectively communicate that love. Both responsibilities require you to take control of the situation from the very beginning, and not leave anything to fate.

Many times it may seem easier to sit back and blame romantic setbacks on your incompatible astrology signs (". . . by the way, what's *your* sign?"), but the real problem is your own inaction. As Shakespeare so wisely put it, "The fault, dear Brutus, is not in our stars, but in ourselves . . ." You, alone, hold the key to your success. You must be determined to turn that key, especially in *this* —the most vital challenge of your entire life.

As the authors of this book, we can reveal the secrets of *what* to do, but only *you* can actually *do* it. Even at this early stage of the book, adopt the motto, "If it's to be, it's up to me!"

LOVE TACTIC #7 Be First To Show Interest In The Other

One of the most helpful facts about human nature is that we most often take notice of, and feel attracted to, people who appear to have a genuine interest in *us*! This is what makes your heart skip a beat, for example, when you catch someone looking at you across a crowded room. *All* of us are susceptible to such kinds of attention. *The best way to favorably impress someone is not by telling them marvelous things about yourself, but by letting them know that you are favorably impressed by them.*

People are reactive creatures, similar to mirrors. Are you aware that many of our attitudes and, indeed, our behaviors toward others are greatly determined by the way others treat us *first?* So the way we feel about others is generally a reflection of the way we think others feel about us!

For example, who do you usually smile at? Yes, those who smile at you first! Also, don't you tend to dislike anyone whom you suspect may secretly dislike you? The most important revelation of all, however, is the realization that you *love* those whom you truly believe *love you!*

The secret, then, to winning someone's love is to first convince him or her of your real, genuine love *for them!* If you want to succeed at love, you'll have to be more than just a mirror. You must *act*, not *react!* You want love to flow *from* you, not merely to be reflected *by* you! This requires patience and self-mastery, which are the ultimate keys to winning someone you want.

Too often in life we sit back and wait for "Mr. or Ms. Right" to come along and show us how much they care, before we are willing to commit ourselves to care back. But there's something we should realize. Everybody does the same thing! Nobody (or very few people, anyway) seems to want to be the one to lead out because of the pain and effort that must be invested.

If you're simply waiting around for your dream person to show up, you could have a very long wait! But it's not necessary to leave your love life to fate. Take advantage of your opportunities! There's a whole world of people out there waiting for you to sweep them off their feet, if you simply have the courage to take the first step.

Showing interest in the other person *first* means being the first to: (1) smile, (2) make eye contact and acknowledge them, (3) extend a vocal greeting, (4) try to engage the other person in conversation, and (5) suggest the possibility of getting together for some sort of date. *Don't give up, even if there is no immediate response.*

Taking a visible interest in the other person is the *first* step to winning their heart. It immediately fills their need for attention (and *everyone* needs attention!), and paves the way for future progress. But, remember, it does not insure a positive response right away. That will come in time. Meanwhile, continue to show interest as you develop your skills in the more advanced techniques.

LOVE TACTIC #8 Go For One Date At A Time

QUESTION: How do you eat an elephant?
ANSWER: One bite at a time.

QUESTION: How do you win someone's heart?
ANSWER: One *date* at a time.

As soon as you have gained someone's attention by showing enough interest, it's time to begin building a relationship. This is done by spending exclusive blocks of time together, commonly known as "dates." A date is simply an opportunity to interact with the one you want on a personal level—one on one.

The first date can be very uncomfortable for both parties. This is because it is generally exploratory. You're getting to know the other person, and learning about their likes, dislikes, idiosyncrasies, or other things that you didn't know before. This can make the first date very interesting. Be yourself, but don't start revealing your faults and self-doubts. We all have these, of course, but you want the other person to leave with a warm feeling of having spent an enjoyable evening with a person who is confident.

Something magical happens when human beings spend time together. They grow on each other. There is a psychologically-binding effect. It appears that magnetic forces between people are more real than is commonly believed!

However, don't betray your anxiousness to tie up the social calendar of the one you want! It's dangerous to ask for more than one date at a time. This can frighten off a potential sweetheart before the binding effect has even begun. At the same time, don't settle for less than a real date. Don't believe that a relationship can grow just by seeing someone every day at class, work, or in some other neutral setting. This won't provide enough electricity to adequately charge the relationship.

So set your sights on that first date. Work for it, and it alone, until you succeed in getting it. No more, no less. Then, *after* completing a date and giving it a little time to be digested, go for another one. Don't push for too much commitment at once. By focusing on one date at a time, you'll actually be building the relationship (at a rate slow enough to keep from chasing away the one you want).

There is a story recounted about an Arab sheik who was once making a journey to a distant city. He had to travel through an extensive desert to get there. While on his way, a terrible windstorm came up and he was forced to set up his small traveling tent for shelter. The wind was furious and the sand beat wildly upon the outer covering of his tent, but he was safe and snug within. Suddenly he heard a pleading voice from outside. It was the voice of his camel.

"Oh please, kind master, " the camel asked, "the wind is so harsh and the beating sand so unrelenting, may I just shelter my mouth and nose from the storm by placing them in the safety of the tent through the tent door?"

The sheik was touched by the humble nature of his faithful camel's request. He thought, "Surely my faithful servant, who carries me so tirelessly and without complaint through scorching desert sand, deserves some respite from these savage winds?" So he permitted him to put his nose and mouth just inside the tent door.

After awhile, the camel said, "Oh master, thank you, kind sir, for the relief you afford me by your goodness and mercy. Is it possible I might also shelter my eyes from the stinging sands . . . ?"

To make a long story short, the sheik eventually found himself out in the violent sandstorm, wondering how he had allowed himself to change places with the camel! The answer: The camel kept his requests for favors surprisingly simple and humble. The smaller the request, the harder it is to deny!

So it is in developing a relationship. You must spend time with the person, *one on one*, to build it properly. This requires many dates, but only ask for one date at a time. Furthermore, if the one you want seems hesitant to grant you time even for a single date, be creative. Think of something you can ask the person to do with you, even if it involves as little as fifteen minutes! For example, you can ask them to let you take them out for a "quickie" ice cream cone later on in the evening, with a promise that you'll have them back home before they know it! Who could be so cold-hearted as to refuse this humble request? Little by little, you'll surely reach your goal.

WHO ASKS WHOM?

A common mistake many people make is to try to get the other person to ask *them* out! One young woman told of meeting a guy at work who really "rang her chimes" like nobody before. He quickly became the one she wanted. She tried to make it obvious she was interested in him. Although he was very nice to her at work, he seemed to ignore the hint and never asked her for a date.

At that point she realized that, in order for the relationship to progress, they needed to go out together. However, she incorrectly concluded that the only way to accomplish this was to entice *him* into taking the first step. So she wrote him a note saying (in effect), "Larry, I've come to appreciate your friendship a great deal and would like to get to know you better." She then signed her name and phone number, obviously hoping that *he* would take the first step and ask *her* out.

That's not the way to do it. Once you decide that this is the person you want, make up your mind to take responsibility for the relationship and risk doing the asking. Trying to shift this responsibility to the other party is *not* the way to succeed. As you might have suspected, "Larry" never even mentioned receiving her note. So she wound up feeling worse than before she sent it!

TAKING THE FIRST STEP . . .

Developing a relationship is kind of like learning to walk. Don't worry about anything other than that first step. If you try to get too far ahead of yourself, you'll trip and fall.

But sometimes, even when you're just concentrating on one step at a time, that one step (the first date) can prove awfully elusive. It doesn't matter! Don't be deterred! You won't get anywhere without the first step. So just make up your mind that you'll work for that first date until you get it. Anyone with a fair amount of dating experience will tell you that things don't always fall into place. Even the most desirable people encounter obstacles. So try not to take it personally.

BE LIKE IKE

Former president Dwight D. Eisenhower experienced the same frustration when trying to get a date with the one he wanted back in his single days. His dream girl told him she was booked up, not only for the *next* weekend, but for the *next three weekends!*

Now the average guy might have taken the hint and given up. But Dwight wasn't your average guy, and he chose to *act* rather than *react!* He was determined to get that one date and waited until Mamie finally said "yes" for the fourth weekend. The rest is history!

STEP BY STEP

Remember that even though the first date is not always easy to get, sometimes it *does* come easily. Then it may be the *follow-up* date that's hard to obtain! Or they may *both* prove elusive! Or . . .whatever! Just keep in mind that the most important date for you to concentrate on getting right now is *the next one!* Eventually, if you keep concentrating on moving one step at a time (all the while applying the other tactics is this book), resistance will melt and the one you want will finally become like putty in your hands! The beginning of any project is always the hardest part. A wise man once said, "That which we persist in doing becomes easier. Not that the nature of the thing has changed, but our ability to *do* has increased!"

LOVE TACTIC #9 Avoid Being Defensive

The most difficult part of being the first person to extend ourselves in a relationship and show interest in the other is that it leaves us extremely vulnerable. If the one we want shows no indication of reciprocating our friendship, it leaves us feeling very foolish.

When this happens, our first impulse is to take quick action. We immediately try to cover up our foolishness and redeem as much of our pride as possible. How do we do this? Generally, we'll withdraw from the contest or, even worse, try to take some punitive action toward the one who has rejected us. For example, we might bitterly snub the person or speak badly of them to others. This kind of defensive behavior only backfires on us, though, and makes the situation worse. What many people never realize is that rejection can almost always be overcome through patience and endurance. This is accomplished by continuing to meet your prospective loved one's basic needs for attention, understanding, acceptance, appreciation, and affection even though they may be neglecting yours. It takes courage and fortitude to be a true and unconditional friend to others, but it pays off in the end!

Lord Melbourne once said, "Neither man nor woman can be worth anything until they have discovered they are fools . . . (and) the sooner the discovery is made the better, as there is more time and power for taking advantage of it." So don't be afraid to look foolish! This fear only paralyzes our ability to reach out to others. And only by reaching out consistently can we maximize the level of trust others will feel for us. There is no shame in rejection! Endure it well! All great human beings have gone through it and, interestingly enough, usually in an amount proportionate to their greatness!

By allowing ourselves to remain open and vulnerable to another human being, even in the face of rejection and feeling foolish, we show our sincerity and true greatness of character. This will persuade others to become similarly open with *us*.

On the other hand, becoming defensive when someone hurts you by not responding to your attention is certainly not the answer. It only reinforces their distant attitude and makes the other person feel justified in their initial standoffishness towards us. By exhibiting a sort of "If-you-don't-want-me-then-I-don't-want-you" type of attitude, we demonstrate very clearly that our ability to be a true friend is shallow. Deep down, the one you want senses their need for someone with *staying power*, someone who will stick with them *in spite of themselves*, and love them even when they act unlovable. So if the other person is resisting, you have a better chance of defusing it with non-defensive behavior. Don't fight fire with fire, or else you might wind up burning down the whole house! Drown resistance with waters of acceptance and love. A few years ago the words of a popular song said, "Love is surrender." What the song is really saying is that sincere caring can only be conveyed after one has surrendered his or her ego and false pride. Make the effort to achieve unconditional friendship and stick with it, even if the going gets tough. Don't get defensive just because the sincerity of the love you extend doesn't seem to sufficiently impress itself upon someone's heart when you first offer it.

RECOVERING FROM REJECTION

No matter who you are, you're going to experience some degree of rejection in trying to win someone's heart. If not in the very beginning, it'll happen at some point down the road. Try not to let this shake you. For heaven's sake, don't resort to negative reactions towards the one you want when you experience any of this rejection! You might comfort your wounded ego a bit, but it'll cost you a good opportunity to build a successful relationship. Great victories in romance are always accompanied by a little pain along the way. No pain, no gain. No war was ever won without losing a few battles along the way, so you mustn't become overly discouraged and give up the fight just because today's struggle seemed to end in defeat. Remember, "You're not beat until you quit!" And, friend, we've got news for you: You're just getting started!

Do you remember our saying that people are like mirrors? It still applies here. Be confident that, eventually, whatever attitudes you send out will come home again. Putting up defensive barriers will only encourage others to maintain them as well. Instead, counter their apathetic response with renewed love, kindness, and attention. Continue to be positive even if they react negatively. Return good for evil, as it says in the

Bible. Let down your defensive barriers. Don't provide others with any ammunition to justify keeping theirs up, and in time you'll find them letting theirs down, too! As philosopher Erich Fromm so aptly observed, falling in love is actually just "the sudden collapse of barriers" between two people.

Allowing yourself to become vulnerable to another human being shows that you care more about the *person* than their actual reactions to you. Over an extended period of time, this type of treatment is guaranteed to produce positive changes in that person's observable behavior towards *you!*

4
Making Time An Ally

Principle: The longer the amount of time a relationship has to grow and mature, the stronger the bonds of emotional attachment two people will feel for each other.

James Thurber once said, "Love is what you've been through with somebody." A little solemn reflection on that statement would soon bring nods of agreement from any thoughtful human being. Of course, we love those with whom we have *shared life itself!* And the more of life we've shared, the deeper the love runs! Can there be any greater bonds of emotional attachment, for example, than those which exist between the remaining members of an old battle-seasoned war battalion? And what exactly knits those families so close together, whose personalities and temperaments would not otherwise so naturally incline the group? It is *shared experience*—the good and the bad! The more they've been through together, the stronger the bond! Ask anyone widowed after 50 years of marriage about this principle and they'll be able to fill you in!

Day by day, little by little, the threads of experience which people share with one another become like strands of a spider's web carefully being spun around them, binding them ever so imperceptibly closer to one another that they don't realize it until they make their first efforts to sever the relationship. Their success in walking away free and clear at that time depends a great deal upon how much experience has been shared between them by then. And of course *that*, in turn, depends upon how much *time* has been allowed for the experience to occur. The more time the relationship has had a chance to grow, generally speaking, the stronger it will be. It was George Washington who said, "Friendship is a plant of *slow* growth."

LOVE TACTIC #10 Take Your Time (Go Slowly)

Marriage experts state that, on the average, the strongest and happiest marriages appear to be those where the couples took at least a year to get to know each other before tying the knot. Consider the example of Theodore Roosevelt (who was known for his strong passions). He took a year and a half to develop a good, strong relationship with his sweetheart. Afterwards, he boasted that his worshipful adoration of her knew almost no limits! And this, in spite of the fact that she held him at bay—practically at arm's length—throughout the whole blossoming relationship!

Had she been too quick to express a willingness to commit herself to him, either by spoken word or through physical affection, his appreciation for her would certainly not have been as great. In fact, it's likely that his anxiousness was the very thing that kept her hesitant, until she finally "broke down" and fell for him.

Theodore Roosevelt understood the frustration of taking it slow in winning the one he wanted. Almost from the moment he met her, he knew she was the girl for him. He vowed in the privacy of his journal "that win her I would, if it were possible." Still, their relationship took a year and a half to grow sufficiently strong for her to return his affection.

Have you ever tried to rush a budding romance along too quickly? This is a very common mistake. Since relationships grow stronger with the passing of time, the trick to succeeding is to try and keep the friendship developing as long as possible at first, *without frightening off a potential lover!* Unfortunately, what most of us do instead is to try to extract some sort of commitment from the one we want at the earliest possible moment. This can seem threatening and ominous. Why? It makes people feel like they're being backed into a corner before they're ready, making them anxious to find an escape. If people are allowed to progress at their own pace, however, the natural course of their emotional growth will lead them to actually feel comfortable about making such a commitment.

Compare winning the one you want to going fishing. When you throw your hook into the water and feel that first nibble, you can't jerk the line too quickly. Sure, it's a temptation to try to pull it in right away! You don't want to take a chance on its swimming away. But if you act *too* quickly, you'll wind up pulling the hook right out of the fish's mouth and losing it completely! This is because the hook needs time to work itself into the mouth and become securely imbedded there. Given enough time, the fish will do most of the work for you, as long as you supply the hook and the bait! So give your lure enough time to work its magic in love, as well! Your human "fish" will bite the bait and become firmly attached to your hook! Do you see the analogy? Make sure the relationship is good and strong before you begin to "reel in" your sweetheart.

FEAR OF COMMITMENTS

Why do people resist getting involved in relationships? Is it love they are running from? Actually, no! People run from making commitments, *not* from being loved! It's only when they start to feel obligated by accepting your love that they'll turn it away. And when we hint that we're including someone in our future plans, the natural human instinct is for them to run as fast and far away as possible!

There was once a young man who fell into a deceptive life of fraud. He had a number of aliases he used as he traveled around the country. During one particular journey he met a girl, and though at first he deceived her and took advantage of her gullibility as he had many others, he soon realized he felt differently about her. He found himself falling in love and felt a strong desire to "go straight" and marry her. Although this would mean completely changing his lifestyle, there was no doubt in his mind that it was what he wanted.

He went to her, made a complete confession, and asked her to marry him. However, it was such a shock to her that instead she called the police! He had no choice but to quickly hop on a plane and get away. He didn't have much time to mourn his loss as he was making his escape.

The Great Realization

Later on in the airplane, though, the young man had an interesting introspective experience. He knew he felt something inside, but couldn't really identify the emotion. Only six hours before, he had wanted to marry this girl more than he had ever wanted anything in his entire life. Now there was no hope of that ever happening. Yet, what was it he was feeling? It wasn't really disappointment. It wasn't anger . . . and then it dawned on him! It was *relief!* For in spite of the fact that he *had* wanted to marry her, the truth was that he was *also very glad now that he didn't have to!* He was relieved that forces beyond his control had emancipated his heart, so that he was no longer bound by any feelings of emotional attachment or obligation. He felt a new appreciation and, indeed, exhilaration for his new-found sense of freedom.

The truth of the matter is, *it's common to feel two conflicting desires at the same time.* One is usually just a little stronger than the other, so that's the one we're most aware of. On the one hand we desire to be free and uncommitted, while on the other hand we yearn to belong to someone. So, while trying to win someone's heart, *you can't ignore their ever-present desire to remain free* (even though at times it may be hidden from view). This points out the wisdom of going slowly. You don't want to scare someone off before he or she is ready for a commitment!

How do you succeed in this? By being slow about revealing your anxiousness to see the one you want all the time. Let the person think that you have only limited intentions of getting together again in the future—possibly one or two dates, but nothing more. This is called "keeping from getting too serious." It doesn't mean that you should stop paying attention to the person. It just means that you should not let the person feel too sure of your long-range intentions.

If a person is going to be comfortable seeing you, you can't threaten their freedom. Everyone has a personal need for emotional breathing space. They must not be given reason to believe that you are expecting them to share their life and future with you. Otherwise, like a person who is choking and fighting for air, the person may desperately seek to escape you.

As long as you keep a person believing that the relationship is merely casual, time will be on your side. Meanwhile, the subconscious process of emotional bonding will continue to bind their heart more closely to yours!

Avoid Impatience

Let's say you're trying to do the right thing. You're trying to take your time in developing the relationship before introducing the element of passion. But then an unexpected turn of events occurs. Someone else starts moving in on your guy or girl! You'll undoubtedly get spooked by this new competition and feel like you've got to hurry. It's natural to feel that if you don't get moving and "sew this one up" for yourself right away, you might lose them permanently!

Don't panic! Remember the story of the tortoise and the hare who decided to have a race? Aesop tells how the hare seemed to have the race won every step of the way. However, the tortoise continued plodding along, never giving up, and never deviating from his proper course. Yes, there must have been times when he thought, "Why bother?," since his rival seemed to have the inside track. But in the end, his relentless, "slow but sure" method turned out to be the quickest and the best! People often spend years unwittingly sabotaging one relationship after another by rushing romance, when they could have exercised patience just once (for, say, only three or four months) by developing a solid friendship *first*, and then been happily married today!

What if rivals do come on the scene? What if they try to quickly introduce romance into their relationship with the one *you* want? Although they may appear to be successful at first, they'll be creating a flaw in the foundation of their relationship which will, in time, become all too evident. They're moving too fast. This can actually work to your advantage if, like the tortoise in Aesop's fable, you keep building your relationship in an unhurried and meaningful way!

Your rivals will experience obstacles. They always do. And when that happens, they'll pay the price of not having built a good solid foundation of pure friendship first. By then, you'll be ready to step in and take over! When the one you want is feeling the need for someone who really cares about them and loves them unconditionally, you'll be there ready to pick up the pieces and carry the person across the finish line!

You'll have your romance, too. But it will occur at the proper time—later—and will be all the more powerful for your having waited!

LOVE TACTIC #11 Be Attentive On A Regular Basis

In *The Little Prince*, by Antoine de Saint-Exupery, the importance of showing regular, almost clock-regulated, attention to someone you'd like to win was clearly demonstrated. In this classic allegorical commentary on love, a lonely but skeptical fox meets a little prince who is out "looking for friends." The fox, realizing that he, too, would like a friend (but also very aware of his own suspicious nature), pleads for the little prince to undertake the task of taming him. But the prince doesn't know how to go about it and asks the fox what steps he should take to accomplish such a feat.

The fox, although bound to obey his instincts, also has a clear understanding of how to get around them. So he explains to the prince that he must expect to exercise great patience in this process. He instructs the prince to sit down at a distance from him in a field of grass, just to observe him for awhile. (He knows that this will gratify his need for attention, while not alarming his sense of freedom.)

Admitting his own apprehensiveness, the fox warns the little prince that even though it may not appear obvious, he will actually be very aware of the prince's presence, ever watching him out of the corner of his eye. However, he further explains that as long as the prince doesn't make any sudden, quick movements in his effort to tame him, and as long as he will return and sit a little closer each day (so as to condition the fox to expect his attentions on a regular basis), the time will come when a relationship will begin to develop. The fox adds that, by coming at the same time each day, the pleasure of his anticipation will be enhanced as the appointed hour draws nigh.

How does this apply to you? In your efforts to "tame" the one you want and win his or her heart, *show attention on a regular basis!* Condition the one you want to expect your presence regularly, even though initially this intrusion into their world may be viewed skeptically "out of the corner of their eye." In time, if you don't make any rash or indiscreet efforts to "capture" the object of your affections, they will find themselves becoming a bit curious towards you and even anticipate your next appearance with some degree of subconscious gladness!

If you begin by making your presence felt in a person's life only once or twice a week, that's fine. But make sure you are regular enough about it so that the person will notice if you don't show up sometime. In time, people develop acceptance of anything that occurs regularly in their lives. So again, take your time in building a relationship, but be *regular!*

BECOME A HABIT

Nothing is quite as powerful as the force of habit in influencing someone's behavior. No tool is more useful in getting someone to do what we want. But can a person actually become conditioned to feel *comfortable* in your presence? The answer is *yes!*

The famous Russian scientist Ivan Pavlov did much to demonstrate the effects of conditioning on living creatures through his "salivating dog" experiments. They came about after noticing that his dog would salivate a great deal more than usual when he was fed. He wondered if the dog could be programmed to produce the same effect, even without the presence of food. So Pavlov began to ring a bell each time food was brought to the dog. This regular pairing of events was continued for quite some time. Then the dog was observed when the bell was rung by itself, without the accompaniment of food. Guess what? The dog salivated with the same anticipatory excitement as if it had just been presented with a juicy steak!

People can have similar experiences, sometimes without even realizing it. (That doesn't mean the one you want will "salivate" at the mere thought of you. Or, who knows, maybe they will!) But if you show attention to the one you want through regular telephone calls, visits, and doing things together, he or she will subconsciously get used to receiving regular attention from you. Where does this lead? The person will become accustomed to feeling good each time they are in your presence, and begin to subconsciously look forward to your next meeting!

LOVE TACTIC #12 Be Persistent

It's not easy to keep showing attention to someone who just seems to want to brush you off. However, don't give up prematurely! Any act of goodness or friendship extended towards another always makes an impression, even if it's not an immediate one. Every such exertion towards the one you want will bring you one step closer to triumph in winning that person's heart.

One of Aesop's more famous stories involves a crow who was dying of thirst. This crow came upon an abandoned pitcher. Once it had been filled with water, but now it was only partially full. The crow put his beak into the pitcher, but found that he couldn't reach down far enough to get to the life-saving liquid. At first he seemed destined to die of dehydration, with water (ironically) only inches away.

But then an idea popped into his head. The crow found a pebble nearby and dropped it into the pitcher. Looking in, the water didn't look any closer, but the situation was desperate, so he resumed the process. He found another pebble and then another. About to die of thirst, he noticed that at last the water was close enough to the top for him to get a drink.

Giving someone attention is like putting pebbles into the pitcher of water. Human beings have an unquenchable thirst for attention. This compelling emotional need must be met continuously, and thus serves as an extremely potent psychological reward. Whether people seem affected by it or not, *they are!*

At first you may not have any visible indication that the attention you are giving is accomplishing something, but rest assured that *it is!* Keep trying. Whatever time and attention you invest in a relationship will ultimately yield a most worthwhile return. If you quit too soon, though, you'll deprive yourself of the ultimate reciprocation of love that would inevitably be yours!

DELAYED REACTION

Another reason why persistence is so important is the *delayed reaction effect*. Realize that you're trying to get the object of your affections to warm up to you. Often, the desired response will come, but not immediately enough to see the direct correlation between your action and the response.

Let's say, for example, that Jim has met Susan, who really strikes his fancy. He'd like to become much better acquainted with her. Imagine what might happen if he showed a great deal of enthusiasm in one of their first encounters:

JIM: "Hello, Susan! Why, what a surprise it is to bump into you here! Do you come here often? I'm here twice a week and don't remember ever seeing you in here before . . ."

Although Susan does remember Jim, she has never really spoken to him before on a familiar basis. Finding herself caught unexpectedly off guard, she has a hard time regaining her composure. She tries to respond without getting herself involved too deeply in a situation she has not yet been able to completely evaluate. So she unintentionally comes across as definitely uninterested.

SUSAN: ". . . er, hi. Uh, no, not usually . . ."

Jim notices Susan's lack of enthusiasm right away. He tries his best to get her interested anyway, with a warm smile and further attempts at conversation.

JIM: "Have you seen Bill Smith or Jan Green lately? I don't think I've talked to them since the night I met you. I've been wondering what they've been up to lately . . ."

But his attempts are in vain. It soon becomes all too apparent to Jim that Susan does not share his interest in becoming better friends.

SUSAN: "No, I haven't seen them, either. Well, I'd better be running along . . ."

JIM: (still smiling and acting enthusiastic, but feeling like a jerk): "Well, it's been real nice running into you! Tell everybody 'hi' for me if you see them before I do. Goodnight!"

SUSAN (feeling relieved that this unexpected encounter is ending quickly enough, but not wanting to risk prolonging it by any show of reciprocated enthusiasm): "Uh, yeah . . . sure . . . Goodnight . . ."

Afterwards, Jim thinks to himself, "Well, it's obvious enough she's not interested in getting to know *me!* I sure made a fool of myself on that one. Now it looks as though I like her and she's just going to give me the cold-shoulder. Well, I sure won't make *that* mistake again. I can tell when I'm not wanted!"

Meanwhile, Susan has now had some time to emotionally digest the experience she's just been through. To her surprise, she finds she even enjoyed it. "My, he was nice!" she thinks to herself. "And what a nice smile! I wonder if he could possibly be interested in *me?* Well, I'm certainly going to have to take advantage of the situation, the next time the opportunity presents itself, and somehow get to know him *better!*"

In most cases, though, Susan's resolution is already too late. The one who was initially interested has already decided to become more cool and distant (and less vulnerable) in any future encounters with the person who failed to respond right away. What happens when Jim and Susan meet again?

SUSAN: "Hello Jim! What a coincidence bumping into you twice in one week!" (Actually, by this time Susan has come here on purpose, hoping for just such a coincidence.) "I guess it's fate, huh?"

JIM (determined not to play the fool again): "Guess so. Well, I better run. See ya . . ."

This time Jim goes away feeling a lot less foolish, but Susan is more convinced than ever that "you can't trust a man. One day he acts interested and the next day he acts like he could care less!" And thus another potentially great relationship goes down the tubes.

All this can be avoided, however. Decide that you'll stick it out and do the right thing, regardless of the lack of apparent reciprocation from the one you want. Have some faith that the tactics you're learning in this book will work if you give them time. If you're willing to put them to the test, they won't let you down!

5

Pacifying Their Fears and Gaining Their Trust

Principle: People have a subconscious need to stay free and emotionally uncommitted. Therefore, they will go to great lengths to avoid circumstances which threaten to limit that freedom.

It is extremely important to exercise restraint when sharing your hopes and dreams with the one you want. There are some things you need to keep to yourself! Anytime you start to let on that your future happiness is hinging *on them*, particularly by your verbal intimations of this, they will begin to feel trapped. Sensing the responsibility being placed on them before they've decided they want it, their instinctive reaction will be to get out of the situation before they get in even deeper.

On the other hand, if you keep your intentions to yourself, you can keep the relationship developing while the bonds of attachment grow ever stronger. It may seem silly not to *talk* about something which, in other ways, may appear so obvious, but you'll be surprised how easily the one you want will accommodate your charade. It is the least intimidating approach for *both* of you. People want to *fall* in love of their own volition, and *not be pushed*. We agree with Thomas Hardy's assessment that, "A lover without discretion is no lover at all." Blabbing blows everything. If you can't maintain your own confidences, after all, how could another ever have trust in you to keep *theirs?* Mature persons of wisdom and experience know enough to keep their motives to themselves. It does no good to disclose one's intentions in the delicate early stages of romance, as it has the irrepressible tendency to drive the one you want away from you.

LOVE TACTIC #13 Show You Care, But Don't Say It!

Not long ago a young woman expressed to one of the authors her aversion to any more "game playing" in her life. She said all she ever wanted again from romance was someone who would sincerely care for her and "lay it on the line." She felt that she could emotionally respond to this kind of openness and candor, though she was told that such could not be the case. It was explained that even though she might sincerely believe she could get excited about such a person, human experience indicated that she would feel differently if it actually came to pass.

A few weeks after this conversation the principle was clearly demonstrated to her. A very eligible young bachelor came knocking at her door and pretty much swept her off her feet—for a few days. She soon had to admit that her new suitor was treating her exactly as she had said she wanted to be treated. However, his openness in talking about their future together was scaring her to death!

The relationship was much too stressful for her. Within a few days after realizing that she wasn't feeling the way she had hoped she would, she terminated the relationship (and, unfortunately, broke an innocent man's heart). Although she felt guilty about hurting such a wonderful guy, the relief she experienced upon breaking off the relationship only reinforced her belief that it was not "right."

Could this relationship have worked out? It very well might have, if the young bachelor had only been wise enough to realize the importance of holding back any talk of "them" and "their future." Such conversation contains too many implied expectations of commitment. Instead of creating stress for the young woman, her hopeful suitor would have been better off playing it cool in the beginning. As long as stress is present in a relationship, communication will be inhibited. This makes it difficult for a relationship to grow. What reasonable way is there to keep a relationship as non-threatening as possible? *Avoid talk that implies commitment to one another!*

Let's be candid here. We all know you have serious intentions, or you wouldn't be reading this book in the first place! *But don't go talking about them!* It's o.k. to *show you care through your actions, but show a little inconsistency when it comes to expressing it!* Don't say it! Don't wear your heart on your sleeve! Whatever you do, don't let your conversation indicate that your present or future happiness depends on the person's reciprocation of your feelings. Don't let the person know that your future plans are beginning to include him or her. This will scare the person off.

SHOW, DON'T TELL

Don't verbalize your feelings. Hold back, especially in the first few months of active dating. Some things in life are better left unsaid. This is especially true in romance. It's o.k. to show that you care. It's o.k. for the one you want to even become a bit *suspicious* that you *might* care. *But no confirmations, please!* Don't *say* it at this early stage! Don't verbally confirm any suspicions they may have until much, much later on in the relationship. (This goes for written communication as well as the spoken word. Sending little cards, notes, and letters that hint your love will only sabotage your efforts to really win someone's heart. This will be one of the most difficult acts for most readers to refrain from, but will richly reward those with enough self-control to refrain.)

People feel trapped and cornered by premature romantic confessions. However obvious your devotion might otherwise seem, it remains non-threatening until you start talking about it. Once you make a verbal confession of your love, however, any continued cooperation from the one you want would be a subtle acknowledgement of that person's commitment to you. They will be faced, then, with the sad choice of accepting your love and surrendering their freedom, or shutting you out of their life. And there is little question which it will be! They are not about to make any permanent commitments to you until they are good and "hooked!"

Remember, people do not run from your love. *They run from getting committed to something they're not yet sure of.* So unless sufficient time has elapsed to allow the other person's feelings to grow and become very strong, any threat to their freedom will produce psychological barriers and cause the person to start avoiding contact with you.

BECOMING ADDICTED TO LOVE

Many psychologists and counselors have described being in love as a type of addiction. In fact, there is some evidence that the pleasurable physical symptoms accompanying romantic love, such as increased heartbeat, sweaty palms, and a feeling of euphoric infatuation, actually do result from the release of phenylethylamine in the brain when the appropriate psychological and emotional responses are triggered.

With this understanding, then, of how love can affect us in a very real way like an addiction, consider the following analogy: When a drug pusher is trying to get someone hooked, how does he go about it? Does he walk up to a potential client and say, "Hi, wanna get hooked?" Of course not! He must be much more subtle than that! Nobody starts out with the intention of getting themselves hooked. And this is just as true of romantic love! Do people jump at opportunities to surrender their freedom? No, but people do feel drawn to situations that produce pleasurable feelings in them. And it's only when someone becomes *convinced* that the trade-off is worth it that they are willing to give up some of their freedom.

So a pusher must be subtle, and should not talk about the long-term *cost*, but rather the immediate *benefits*. He doesn't say, "How would you like to spend the rest of your life hopelessly dependent on what I have to offer you?" Who would ever accept such a crazy offer? Instead he says, "Hey, wanna feel good? No cost, man. This one's on me!" And so, gradually—step by step—a dependency is developed.

You should go about winning love from another in a similar fashion. If you start talking about how much you care for the one you want, this will automatically be read as your asking for reciprocation, or "payment." You're giving notice indirectly that you'll be expecting payment from the person in the future, and that can be very frightening to them. Instead, just give the one you want consistent, caring *attention*, without any indications of anything out of the ordinary. Later, once your special someone is good and hooked and there's no chance of losing them, there will be plenty of time to start receiving love in return!

6

Being Irresistably Likable

Principle: The more positive and beneficial the experience someone has when interacting with you, the greater will be that person's desire to continue the association.

Can you get someone you want to *like* you? Even though the human mind will not be forced into anything, it most certainly can be led! And if you know and apply the rules, you can coax any person you choose into enjoying and looking forward to the pleasure of your company.

Countless books have been written on this very subject. Persons of great experience and wisdom all agree: The things you do, the way you treat and act towards others, *do* determine how they think of, and act towards, you! So if you want to be well-liked, follow the guidelines in this chapter.

LOVE TACTIC #14 Light Up!

A grandfather was talking proudly about his grandchildren. Although he made it plain he loved them all, he reluctantly admitted that he was partial to one of them in particular. "I try not to be that way," he explained, "but you know how it is!

We tend to respond to the way others act towards us, and the little guy is always so excited to see me whenever I come around that I can't help myself!"

The same tendency exists in all of us. Whenever you notice that someone is particularly happy and excited to see and talk to you, don't you find yourself feeling emotionally rewarded just for having been there with them?

Did you ever wonder why dogs are such popular pets? It is for this very reason. People love coming home to someone who gets excited to see them, even if it's just a lovable, tail-wagging animal who can't talk.

So learn a lesson from "the little guy" and from "man's best friend." When the one you want comes around, or calls, show some excitement. Light up!

LOVE TACTIC #15 Show Those Pearly Whites (Smile)!

One day, two high school boys were discussing their favorite subject—girls—when they stumbled upon a very important truth. They had both agreed that they wanted a girlfriend with a cute face, and were trying to decide what quality determined "cuteness." Suddenly it dawned on them. "Cuteness" was almost invariably related to the amount of smiling a girl did!

Think about it. Aren't the people who you're most attracted to usually the ones who exhibit bright, happy smiles? You'll find that even the ones who you *aren't* particularly interested in become much more attractive when they smile. Why is a smile so powerful? A smile communicates *love*. It radiates acceptance. And making a person feel we accept them is one of the most effective ways we can influence people.

Try an experiment. Walk past a number of people, glancing at them *without* smiling. Keep a mental tally and notice how many of them respond to you. Then try the same experiment with a similar amount of people, *but this time smile and nod as you pass them.* You'll find that you will get a much more positive and gratifying response in the second experiment. (You may even meet somebody special!) By smiling and nodding you're conveying a very positive impression. You are giving others the feeling that they are worthwhile and special.

Can you imagine how many people go through life never realizing that this is *the most effective key* to being attractive to members of the opposite sex? And it's so simple! Even the most ardent opposition melts away, like morning frost before the sunshine, when we're smiled at. It has been said that people can say or do just about *anything*—and get away with it—as long as they smile when they do it!

No matter what the topic of conversation, a smile can make everything right! If you have a warm genuine smile on your face, and make good eye contact, you'll help that person to feel much more at ease. Later, even if they can't remember what you talked about, they *will* remember *the feeling* they had during the conversation. Remember, it's easy to smile! It's such a powerful, positive tool that you can never use it too much!

A smile says many things. It says you're happy. You're confident. You're feeling secure. It says you enjoy talking to the person you're with, and you like being with them. It shows you want that person to feel comfortable, and that you care enough about them to try and relate.

A would-be lover without a smile is like a warrior going into battle without a weapon. It is indispensable! Armed with a smile, no challenge is too formidable. It is a wise person, indeed, who realizes the importance of including a smile in their romantic arsenal to help them win the one they want!

LOVE TACTIC #16 Speak With Enthusiasm!

Enthusiasm is contagious! It breeds excitement in others! Therefore, it is one of the keys to influencing others in a positive way. Few human beings are immune to its infectious powers. When people are enthusiastic it makes those around them feel happier and more alive than they were before. Because this is a positive experience, it contributes to the bonds of friendship that strengthen people's attachments to each other. So when speaking to the one you want, don't just sit there in a lifeless heap. Put some enthusiasm in your voice! Be a little bit dramatic in your verbal communications.

Remember, people get bored easily. Any effort you make to liven up your conversations will be appreciated by others, whether they readily show it or not. Enthusiasm is a subtle way of *showing* you care, and will endear yourself to any with whom you practice it.

Don't be too sober or serious. It's so much better to have a light, positive attitude about life. Have a good sense of humor and don't be afraid to laugh freely. You'll also find that others will respond more readily to you if you smile and exhibit a sense of humor.

Try to radiate happiness as much as possible. If you're trying to interest somebody in spending time with you, an upbeat, happy attitude is essential. Be animated! Enthusiasm will make you an enjoyable companion to the one you want!

LOVE TACTIC #17 Talk Positively

The difference between an optimist and a pessimist is that the optimist sees a glass of water as half full, and the pessimist sees it as half empty. Since, subconsciously, we would all prefer half a glass of *something* to half a glass of *nothing*, it is usually more rewarding to be in the company of the optimist.

No matter where you go in life, or what situations you encounter, you'll have opportunities to judge for yourself how full the glass is. Life is full of plights and predicaments. How you share your view of your circumstances with others will determine the degree to which your company will be enjoyed. If you have a positive outlook, the one you want (not to mention everyone else with whom you come in contact) will subconsciously value your friendship more dearly. It pays to talk positively!

Single college students, when polled about desirable character traits they would like in a future mate, have consistently rated "sense of humor" high on their lists. Yet when pressed for a more precise definition of what this actually means to them, respondents indicate that the term does *not* refer to the ability to tell jokes effectively! Rather, it is the ability to look on the bright side of things—the willingness to laugh at a hopeless situation. People who do this are uplifting to be around and, whether they realize it or not, quietly endear themselves to others. It is emotionally rewarding to be in their presence.

LOVE TACTIC #18 Discuss The Other Person's Interests

It is a fact that most people do not have great confidence in their abilities to carry on a conversation. Yet, communication with others remains a basic human need. So if you want your friendship to be highly valued and sought after, you must learn how to help the one you want to be comfortable talking with you.

Surprisingly, the key is *not* necessarily having an extensive knowledge of many subjects. Rather, it is a willingness to *let the other person do most of the talking*, on any subject *they* are interested in! You can draw out anybody in this fashion by assuming the position of a sincere student willing to learn from a more informed instructor. Normally, conversation is characterized by a subtle kind of tug-of-war. In the usual exchange, each participant merely waits for the other to stop talking so they can shift the topic back to one more along the lines of their own interests! It is a rare and gratifying experience, for *any* person, when someone else encourages them to keep on talking about what interests them.

How can you best encourage this? By using sincere inquiry and quiet listening. Ask about the other person's goals, accomplishments, experiences, or attitudes. In short, ask about anything and everything *relating to that person*. It is the one subject on which *all people* are experts!

Dale Carnegie once reported the case of a celebrated bigamist who had captured the hearts (and bank accounts!) of twenty-three women. When the bigamist was asked how he had gotten so many women to fall in love with him, he responded that it was no problem at all if he just got the woman to talk about herself. Although there is often more to it than just that, there is no question that encouraging the other person to talk about his or her interests will win them over. Thus, conversing in terms of the other person's interests should be a fundamental technique in your strategy to develop a solid friendship with the one you want!

LOVE TACTIC #19 Use Flattery

Flattery will get you *everywhere!* This is a well-known fact. It is an *extremely* effective way for a person to endear themselves to others. But quite often people hesitate to use it for fear that their gestures of praise will be dismissed as insincere. It's true that most people act suspicious and distrustful when others pay them flagrant, outright compliments. But deep down they are gratefully eating it up, in spite of any outward skepticism. As Paul H. Gilbert put it, flattery is "the art of telling another person exactly what he thinks of himself."

So don't be fooled! When people seem disbelieving of, and resistant to, your flattery, realize that it's *just a show on their part.* Actually, they are deeply affected by it—more than they'd like you to know. The human need for appreciation is stronger than any human ability to resist it. Therefore, your compliments and words of praise will go a long way in building relationships. Be liberal in offering it.

A word of caution, though. Flattery is very potent, like fine perfume. A little bit goes a long way. Sprinkle it around and trust it to do its job. Don't feel the need to pour it on unceasingly just because the recipient doesn't seem to be responding to it. *Too much* flattery may cause your praise to appear unduly suspicious and undermine your genuine sincerity. People tend to put up psychological barriers and become more resistant when they have reason to think they're being "set up" and "put on." But having said that, let us repeat: Your compliments and words of praise will go a long way in building and strengthening relationships. Use flattery. It will make you an enjoyable companion and strengthen your relationship with the one you want.

LOVE TACTIC #20 Understay Your Welcome

It is, of course, well-recognized that by hanging around someone for too long in any given situation, a person can wear out their welcome rather easily. But consider this: If you *understay* your welcome when you're with others, you can actually leave them wanting more of you, *even if they weren't that interested in you to begin with!* This simple, but certain, tactic not only eliminates subconscious resistance to developing a friendship with you, but also creates a positive atmosphere for future get-togethers. People will enjoy your company *more*, as a result of having you available *less!*

So be sensitive as to how much time you spend with the one you want. Depart while things are still going good, even though you're having a good time and may want to stay longer. You be the one who cuts the conversations, the phone calls, the dates, or other encounters a little bit shorter than expected. Just say, "It's time to go . . . ," or, "I've got to get in early . . . ," or just a plain "Goodnight!," but be sure you're the one to initiate it!

Seek out the other person's company, but then also be the first to take leave of them. If you allow the other person to tell you when it's time to go, you will be inadvertently surrendering much of the potential influence of this tactic.

LOVE TACTIC #21 Be Graceful When You're (Temporarily) Rejected

One of the great classic musicals of all time is *The Music Man*, starring Robert Preston and Shirley Jones. In the movie, Preston (as travelling flimflam salesman "Harold Hill") comes to gullible River City, Iowa, with the clear intent (clear to the audience, not so clear to the residents of River City) of swindling the naive townspeople out of their hard-earned money. The scheme necessitates his masquerading as a music professor (hence the film's title). Promising to organize a boys' band, he makes his money by selling band instruments and then skipping town without completing his agreement. In order to pull everything off smoothly, though, the plan requires him to first win the confidence of the townspeople by romancing their local librarian (and part-time music teacher), Marian.

But, as is true of every good love story, there's a hitch. Marian is very suspicious of "Professor" Hill and is not easily romanced. Time after time, he approaches her on the street and cheerfully doffs his hat in an effort to introduce himself to her, but she always gives him the cold-shoulder and walks on by. Still, he remains undaunted.

Most people, when stiffed like that, would respond negatively and defensively. But not the positive-thinking Professor Hill! His vast amount of salesmanship experience had apparently taught him that a positive attitude and smile would ultimately tear down the walls separating the two of them. He responded to her temporary rejection of him with an even bigger smile and a pleasant comeback. And, sure enough, in the end, she succumbed to his charm and was finally won over by him.

Real life is like that, too. Those who are willing to lose some small battles gracefully will wind up winning big wars impressively!

DEALING WITH THE SKIDS

One of the most important things taught in a driver's education class is how to regain control of your vehicle when it starts to slide out of control. "Turn *into* the slide!" students are instructed again and again. So it is with relationships.

Let's say you have a clear idea where you want the relationship to go, but you can feel the person slip-sliding away.

That's not the time to turn towards your goal with even more determination, in hopes the one you want will follow. It won't happen! Instead, you'll throw your whole relationship into a real spin-out! It's better to temporarily "go with the flow," and not seem to resist their efforts to slide off the road. If a person doesn't seem ready to accept the degree of involvement that *you* want, then it's better for you to appear willing to accept the degree *that he or she wants.* In reality, that doesn't mean that you're willing to give up your original plans for the relationship (any more than the driver of a vehicle is willing to slide into a ditch). But sometimes you have to turn in that direction long enough to regain control and gently guide the one you want back to you!

When you get turned down in your request for a date, or brushed off in a conversation, don't turn *off* your charm. Turn it on stronger! *Smile even bigger!* Be willing to bow out temporarily with parting words of kindness and good will. It is this kind of behavior on your part that will convince others that the friendship you offer is genuine, sincere, and worth having. People can't help but love and admire someone who is gracious in the face of apparent defeat. Losing gracefully will subconsciously induce others to be trusting of you in the future. And, remember, love is based on trust!

7

Exhibiting Self-Mastery and Leadership Ability

Principle: People respect, and are subconsciously drawn towards, those who exhibit qualities of aloofness and independence. They are repulsed by those who manifest tendencies to cling.

Obviously, it's important in romance to exhibit very positive and accepting attitudes towards those whom you desire. But you mustn't ever let it appear as though your feelings for them are affecting your decision-making abilities or independence! Remember this: *It's practically impossible for a human being to experience romantic feelings for someone they can manipulate like a puppet!* Thus, if you want to be loved *romantically,* it is of paramount importance that you demonstrate to others that you are an independent, self-respecting person whose wrath they will incur if your goodness is ever taken for granted! Without this element of fear (yes, *fear!*) in a relationship, true romantic love can never fully develop.

If a person feels they can walk on your feelings disrespectfully *and get away with it,* human experience has clearly shown that they will not be stirred up with romantic desire for you. Here, then, are a number of ways to establish your independence and command the respect that is so essential to romantic love.

LOVE TACTIC #22 Plan Out Dates Ahead Of Time

This may be the easiest way to exhibit leadership and demonstrate emotional independence to the one you want. When it comes to dates, *have a plan!* Never give the mistaken impression that you are content to just let things happen to you. Know ahead of time most (if not all) of the details regarding where you're going, what you'll be doing, and how long it will take. Don't leave these things to chance, or it will appear that you're not in control. Have definite objectives and goals in mind for each date, which you have had an active part in outlining. This will demonstrate your ability to act as an independent agent and will earn you the respect of others.

This doesn't mean you should be *selfish!* Always consult with the other person in the planning process. Ask the other person what *they* would like to do. If he or she wants to do something other than what you have in mind, don't be stubborn! You can still demonstrate your active role in the planning by offering options, or at least hearing their ideas and communicating your agreement.

If you're not the person initiating the date, don't remain passive. You still have some say in the outline of events through your power of consent! You may assertively agree or disagree with the events as they've been presented to you. But at least insist on being informed. Remember, showing leadership qualities doesn't necessarily mean you must initiate *everything*. But it does mean that you are made aware of the plan for the date. This insistence will command respect from those you date!

LOVE TACTIC #23 Demonstrate Independent Thinking

What people are actually seeking from romance, whether they

consciously realize it or not, is someone to lean on and draw strength from during life's frightening and distressing moments. Because of this, people are instinctively attracted to those persons who appear emotionally strong themselves, because they'd be most capable of providing such companionship.

Think of a situation where you would need someone to talk to. Maybe you're upset about something, or you're just feeling lonely. Who would you rather talk to? Would you prefer someone who's independent, clear-thinking, and level-headed? Or would you prefer someone anxious to have you make their decisions and do their thinking for them? Be honest, now. Most people are repulsed by such insecurity. Most people are attracted to those who they sense are strong! In short, most people want *to lean*, not *be leaned on!* So it follows that if you want to attract others to you in a long-term relationship, you must demonstrate an ability to do your own thinking and make your own decisions in your associations with others. How can you do this? There are several ways.

SHOWING DECISIVENESS

Be decisive when given choices. When your date asks you what you'd like for dinner, or what movie you'd like to see, respond with some definitiveness (even when such matters appear trivial and you really don't care!). Such opportunities to assert your decision-making abilities mustn't be overlooked!

In dating relationships, many people innocently defer judgment in small matters back to their date. They don't realize that they'd command greater respect, and thus become more desirable, by simply making their own choices.

BENEFITS OF CONTRARINESS

Be contrary, sometimes. Don't always go along with everything your date wants and suggests. You won't be adequately respected if you do. The person mustn't be allowed to receive the mistaken impression that you could be easily led around by them, as if you had a *ring through your nose!*

Make some suggestions of your own at times, even if you'd be perfectly content to let your partner have his or her way all the time. And even if the two of you wind up not doing what you've suggested, it will stick in the other person's mind that you're not just blindly following their every whim. This will automatically enhance your desirability.

GIVING OPINIONS

Speak your mind! There's nothing wrong with offering opinions in a discussion. You may not want your views to seem too outlandish or offending, but at the same time you don't want to come across as an easily-intimidated, browbeaten person with no opinions of your own! The main idea is to speak your mind without concern for whether people will think you are boring or wrong because of it. The "points" you make by exhibiting such an independent attitude will more than compensate for any potential mistakes you might make.

Don't feel that your opinions have to agree with others'. *Be your own person!* Be comfortable saying what you think, even when it is contrary to prevailing thought. Don't be afraid to stand alone! Nothing is more attractive than someone who has the courage to stand up for their convictions.

This does *not* mean, however, that you have to be unpleasant in doing so. It is certainly possible to pleasantly disagree. Never try to force someone else to accept your ideas.

Be honest, open, and forthright. Don't be afraid to manifest independent thinking. It is one of the keys to fulfilling romance!

LOVE TACTIC #24 Communicate Your Personal Destiny

A young man who was having a hard time winning the girl of his dreams sat down after a particularly uninspiring date. "What am I doing wrong?" he wondered. He couldn't quite put his finger on it, but finally concluded that he couldn't go on any longer centering his life around *her*. He decided that, no matter what happened, he was going to maintain the attitude that he still had a special goal in life to accomplish, whether she loved him back or not. If she wanted to accompany him on that mission, she could be part of it. If not, that was fine, too, because he would go on to fulfill it *without her!*

Although his determination was mostly a final attempt to salvage as much of his self-esteem as possible, an amazing turn of events resulted. What happened? His attitude of "I'm going somewhere in life, with or without you!" inadvertently demonstrated his emotional independence to the girl of his dreams and won her love! It's much easier to fall in love with someone who is going somewhere in life regardless of what you do, than it is with someone who you know is basing their entire future on you.

Joan of Arc won the unwavering love and devotion of the battle-smitten armies of fifteenth-century France by exhibiting this very attitude. She once declared to one of her generals, "I will lead the men over the wall." His response was, "Not a man will follow you." But Joan, naturally possessing those same qualities of independence and self-determination that we've been discussing, merely said, "I will not look back to see whether anyone is following or not!"

In your quest for love and devotion, then, be like Joan of Arc! Communicate your intentions to accomplish something worthwhile in life to the one you want, and convey your intention to do it alone, if necessary. Such an attitude will inspire the one you want with desires to follow and be with you!

LOVE TACTIC #25 Be Unpredictable

A prominent psychologist, speaking to an assembly of college students some years ago, remarked that one of the things people need most in their lives to be happy is a little variety. Variety is, indeed, the "spice of life." It provides mental stimulation and keeps us interested in continuing on with life's wearisome struggle. Without it, life becomes dull and uninteresting, and people find themselves easily bored.

Sometimes we fail to realize just how prone human beings are to becoming bored, and thus how easily drawn they will be to someone who shows promise of keeping life interesting. So do the unexpected from time to time! You can hold others' interest simply by never letting them be sure of your next move. This doesn't mean that you won't behave dependably most of the time. It just means that, every once in a while, you will surprise people by doing something a little different from what they are anticipating.

An example? Surprise your special someone with a gift *when they least expect it!* When they think they've got you hooked, *ignore them!* And then, just when they start believing you've stopped caring about them, *drop by for a visit!* Do the unexpected! Be unpredictable! Be nice to them when they're cruel to you, and when they treat you nice, don't be afraid to act a little indifferent. Your ability to keep 'em guessing will be one of your most effective weapons in maintaining their respect for you and winning their love.

How often do you hear people in relationships exclaim, "I just can't figure him (or her) out!"? Isn't it interesting, though, how in every case the one saying this is usually the person in the relationship who is *most hooked?!*

LOVE TACTIC #26 Act Indifferent To Their Opinion Of You

A number of years ago a young man and woman had been seeing each other for awhile and a potential romance was in the offering. The young man had been particularly intrigued by the young woman and the independent attitudes she exhibited. One night, however, she lost much of her appeal when she inadvertently let him know that she was concerned about his opinion of her. It happened rather innocently, really. They had been talking about some trivial matter when she suddenly came out with a rather bold statement of the way she viewed a particular issue. The young man disagreed with her and it must have shown on his face. However, less evident to her observations, he felt himself extremely attracted by the strength of character and the independent aloofness she was showing. At last, he thought, he had found a girl who was his equal in every way!

His sudden fascination was short-lived, however. When the young woman realized that she had said something contrary to the way her suitor believed, she quickly backed down and admitted feeling badly about having expressed herself in such a forthright manner. *Most damaging of all, though, she admitted her concern that the young man might now think less of her for having been so bold!*

Can you see the irony in this? Only a moment before, the young man had begun respecting her more because of her courageous ability to express her feelings without any apparent regard for what he might think of her. But then she became apologetic and blew everything! If she had only continued acting indifferent to his opinion of her, the young man most certainly would have respected her more for it. But when she exhibited a willingness to back down and compromise her independence, *simply to please him,* she lost esteem in his eyes. He couldn't help feeling this way. Respect towards another person is cultivated by one's perception of how independent and aloof they are.

So in your associations with others, *act indifferent to what they appear to think of you (even though you may actually care a great deal)!* Don't admit to them that their opinions of you matter! A recent song asked, "Why did you have to be a heart-breaker, when I was being what you want me to be?" The answer to that question is this: Because you can't have romantic feelings for someone you don't respect, *and you can't respect someone who you know is willing to sacrifice their individuality to suit your opinions.* Romance can only flourish when you manifest a carefree attitude of indifference about the other person's opinion of you. This is a fundamental principle of human behavior!

LOVE TACTIC #27 Don't Fish For Feedback

When caught up in the agonies of romantic pursuit, it's only natural to want to find out where you stand with the one you want. What do they think of you? At times, the urge to seek some sign of reciprocation will become almost too strong to resist. *You mustn't yield, however, to this temptation! Fishing for feedback is definitely detrimental to your romantic health!*

There are two fundamental problems with sending up trial balloons to try to get a reading on someone's romantic feelings about you. First, any feedback you get is, at best, an unreliable indicator of a person's true feelings. Most people don't even know their own minds when it comes to love, so anything they tell you wouldn't necessarily be an accurate indicator of what the person subconsciously feels. It's very possible that a person is *growing* to love you but is not yet consciously aware of it. The transition from a subconscious to a conscious state of love is possible and will inevitably occur if you don't become discouraged and give up prematurely.

Second, probing for emotional attitudes is a hint that you're hoping for reciprocation from the one you want. This, in turn, exposes your emotional fragility. It signals that you're vulnerable to rejection by them and, consequently, are at their mercy! This will diminish their feelings of dutiful respect toward you and undermine the strength of your otherwise growing romance.

Never ask someone, or act concerned about, how they feel towards you, *until you're sure you've already won 'em over!* Seeking for assurances of affection only communicates emotional insecurity on your part and destroys the kind of respect necessary if others are to truly burn with romantic desire for you later on. Ironically, the more aloof you can *appear* about the other person's attitude towards you (at the same time extending yourself to them in true friendship), the more you'll earn their respect and, ultimately, their love!

LOVE TACTIC #28 Express Anger Verbally When The Right Moment Arrives

If you've ever been dumped by someone you wanted and can't remember ever having chastised them somewhere along the way, then you probably lost them unnecessarily! Does this sound strange? Well, it's true, nonetheless! *Showing anger towards the one you want is sometimes necessary for a happy relationship.* Although it's usually best to be agreeable and pleasant when trying to build a relationship, there are times when a sociable complacence is *not* the proper course to pursue. In order to elevate the relationship beyond the level of being "just friends," you need to demonstrate your ability to get angry with the person (even if you have to fake it a little bit)! A good, verbal chewing out is sometimes the only way to show the one you want that you are, after all, independent-minded and worth respecting!

Can you imagine a child growing up without the need for occasional chastisement? Of course not! Having someone on hand to enforce behavioral limits is, in fact, a necessary part of a happy and secure childhood. Well, the same applies to adults. They're just kids themselves, after all, in grown-up bodies. And adults, too, should be put in their proper place from time to time! A future mate will be much happier knowing that you're not afraid to show anger when they get out of line!

Listen to Lee's explanation concerning the difference between Karen, the girl he couldn't live without, and all the previous girls in his life who were incapable of stirring him to that same, high level of devotion: "She's the first girl in my life," he said, "who's ever stood up to me!"

This ability to stand up to the one you want and occasionally tell them off when they abuse your feelings or otherwise take you for granted is an essential key to romantic love. Nobody can really get excited about you if they're not secretly just a little bit afraid of crossing you! This is one of the best-kept secrets of romantic love. Make a note to remember it!

So stand up for your rights and get angry with the one you want, if you really want them to love you! Follow these guidelines, though:

1. Don't scold prematurely. In other words, make sure you have patiently laid a foundation of sufficient selflessness and "long suffering" on your part to justify your right to be angry.

2. Don't get side-tracked fighting about petty, irrelevant issues. The only thing you ever really need to show anger over is any basic disrespect, or lack of regard, for your feelings. (This is the only charge you really ever have any right to bring against them, anyway. You have no right to make yourself their judge on other matters!) Express disappointment in them. Say something like, "Hey, I've taken just about all the lack of consideration I'm going to take! I've given unselfishly and you've just taken it for granted. Well, I refuse to put up with that kind of treatment from *anybody—even you!*"

3. Don't stick around to let the person try and fight with you. Don't argue. State your case, show anger while doing it, *and then depart!* Leave them to their conscience and let your words sink in. Being sucked into a verbal ping-pong match will only weaken the otherwise very powerful effect this tactic can have. You'll be surprised at its power. Remember, *reason* doesn't motivate human beings—*emotion* does! Once you get the emotional pendulum moving, it will eventually swing your way. By employing this tactic, you will incalculably strengthen your sphere of influence with the one you want!

(*Caution:* This tactic will backfire unless strictly used in conjunction with Love Tactic #29: "Show Forgiveness After Expressing Anger.")

LOVE TACTIC #29 Show Forgiveness After Expressing Anger

Yes, you *can* gain a person's respect by being able to stand up to and chastise them when they deserve it! But it's *absolutely essential* that you be the first to demonstrate kind and charitable feelings for them afterwards, if you don't want to destroy the foundation of friendship you've previously established. Human beings are extremely sensitive to chastisement, and the one you want is *no exception*. If you don't take steps to reassure the one you've stood up to that you're still friends, it won't be long before they'll despise you as an enemy! This would be as fatal romantically as to never have been respected in the first place!

Therefore, as soon as your angry words have had a chance to sink in, take steps to show the rebuked person that, although your reaction was strong, you're still loyal. You still care. Don't apologize or act as though your anger wasn't justified. (It most certainly *was*!) This is not the time to back down and start acting like your anger was a mistake. Just seek out the person's company and resume the relationship, completely putting the incident behind you.

The other person will undoubtedly act a bit standoffish at first, even if he or she knows that your anger was justified. Their pride will still be smarting. (After all, the truth can *hurt!*) *But don't you be discouraged!* Just be persistent in renewing the friendship. Soon, amiable feelings will return on their part. It'll become evident that your friendship is unconditional and that you intend to be their *true friend* in spite of any standoffishness they may exhibit. When this happens, your relationship with the one you want will take one of its biggest steps toward romantic fulfillment. It is the same principle by which two kids in junior high become best friends after clearing the air with an after-school fist fight!

8

Inducing Emotional Dependence

---

*Principle: People become emotionally "hooked"
on those persons who can truly satisfy their
never-ending need for human understanding.*

There is a big difference between *loving* and being *in love*. If you *love* someone, you're still in control of your emotional feelings—you still have a choice regarding how you'll allow yourself to feel about, and react towards, that individual. If you've fallen *in love*, however, you're no longer calling the shots. You become hopelessly dependent upon (and at the mercy of) whomever you have allowed yourself to fall for. Remember: The key to winning the one you want is to first get that person to become emotionally dependent *on you*—not the other way around!

Have you ever wondered why it is so common for clients to fall in love with their psychotherapists? It's because there is a very real tendency for people to fall in love with those who satisfy their emotional needs. In an effective counseling session, the client finds that his or her emotional needs for compassionate understanding are being met, perhaps for the first time. They find themselves becoming willingly dependent on their counselor for a continued satisfaction of those needs. They become "hooked" on their therapist.

Likewise, as you learn to satisfy a person's deep-rooted emotional need for understanding, you will in time find them becoming emotionally dependent on *you*. Being successful at love sometimes requires playing the role (to a small degree) of a psychotherapist (and a good one at that!). The better you become at this, the deeper the love that will be felt for you by the one you want. The following tactics will help you to assume that role.

LOVE TACTIC #30 Be There (In Person!)

When Sir Edmund Hillary was asked what compelled him to climb mountains, he responded, "because they're there!" This same principle may be applied to love. The (unromantic, but true) fact is that a person's availability plays a large role in having someone fall in love with them.

The first requirement that must be satisfied, then, is for you to make yourself available to the one you want. You must make your presence *known* and *felt*. This will not always be easy. You mustn't be afraid, though, of "intruding" to some degree into his or her life. Sometimes the greatest love is found, not because we went out and actively sought it, but because somebody pushed it on us at a time when we thought we weren't yet interested. When people buy, it is always from the salesman who was there to sell to them. And when people are ready to fall in love (mark these words very carefully!), *it will always be with someone who is relatively close at hand!*

One enterprising young college student made use of this principle while courting his wife-to-be. He said that even when she wasn't around when he called, he would always leave a message with her roommates so as to keep her constantly aware of his proximity. (Still, he never let her think she had him all sewed up, either! Later, when she'd return his call, he'd be out on a date with someone else!)

So be there for the one you want—even when they don't seem to need or want you! The time will come when they *will* need someone—and you'll be there to step in! Like the patient who has come to depend on his therapist in a time of crisis, the one you want will turn to *you* in their hour of need.

Remember, the underlying message of all advertising is: "If you're in a buying mood, I've got something to sell!" Whether it is an unexpected visit, a quick phone call, or just a note letting the person know you're thinking about them, such small acts of kindness will eventually result in their emotional dependence on you.

The necessity of actually being there in person in order to win the one you want cannot be overemphasized. *Personal, face-to-face contact is vital.* Too often, people try to develop relationships subtly (through the mail, for example) and wonder why it doesn't seem to work. Well, that's the chicken's way out! Building a relationship is no easy task and cannot be accomplished from a distance.

Sure, there are stories of people who met and corresponded by mail at one point in their courtship and are happily married today. But this is only part of the picture. In order for someone to fall in love with you, they've got to get to know you first. Remember, "to know you is to love you," and *getting to know you requires personal, face-to-face contact.*

Why do you think there is such a high incidence of office romances? It's because *work throws people into situations where they have to be together!* This lays the groundwork for further relationship development. You don't have to work with someone before they'll fall in love with you, but you do have to personally spend time with them!

LOVE TACTIC #31 Listen Reflectively

People want someone they can confide in. They really do! They are happiest and function best when there's at least one other person who really knows and understands what they're going through.

And yet, despite this fact, many people seem to have a hard time revealing their true thoughts and feelings to others. How often have you heard a frustrated but caring partner in a rocky relationship lament, "I beg him [her] to tell me what's wrong, but he [she] just clams up and keeps it inside!" Many people find it difficult to open up, even to this kind of sincere prodding.

What can you do to win someone's trust and break down the communication barriers? Start using a method known as *reflective listening*. This technique can be one of the most successful ways to strengthen your relationships with others. Although entire books have been devoted to the particulars of this technique, here we will simply outline the essential keys to listening reflectively. Commit them to memory. Practice them in your relationships with others. You'll immeasurably increase your influence with people in general—and especially with the one you want!

1. *Remain silent while the other person is speaking.* Don't try to interrupt. Let the person talk as long as they want. The more willingness you exhibit to let the other person express himself or herself fully, the more completely you'll help satisfy their emotional need to be understood. This also encourages the person's honesty and openness.

2. *Keep your body still.* Fidgeting conveys impatience and disinterest on your part. You know how important body language is, right? Well, fidgeting can prevent the speaker from revealing what's really on their mind and in their heart.

3. *When the speaker pauses for some acknowledgment that you're really listening and understanding, just nod your head. Restrict your comments to such things as ''Mm-hmm'' or ''Yes, go on . . .''* As one man explained it, "I don't want sympathy or criticism. I just want a listening ear."

4. *Keep your eyes focused on the speaker while he or she is talking.* Not looking at the person implies that you're really not interested in what they're saying. (Think about it. What's the first thing *you* do when you wish a person would shut

up and quit talking?) You can't really expect people to open up to you if they see that you're not truly interested, now can you?

5. *Occasionally, when the person pauses for some response from you, briefly sum up (in your own words, if possible) what you feel they are trying to say.* Try to describe their feelings *even more accurately than they themselves have.* This process will help the speaker to more clearly identify his or her own feelings, while experiencing a sense of unity with you.

    How about an example?

    TIM: "You know, I've had it with the people at my office!"

    TINA: "Go on . . ."

    TIM: "All they ever do anymore is pick, pick, pick on everything I try to do!"

    TINA: "Sounds as if you're upset because the people at work are overly critical."

    TIM: "You got it! They're anxious to jump down my throat for practically nothing, but they never notice anything good that I do."

    TINA: "Kind of like they're quick to criticize you for trivial, unimportant things, while totally overlooking your positive accomplishments?"

    TIM: "That's exactly the way it is!"

    Once you can get the person to respond positively to your summation of their feelings, you can be sure that you're on the right track. You'll be surprised at how anxious people will be to continue opening up to you when you make them feel understood. Believe it or not, this simple technique can keep people talking about themselves and their feelings for hours! It even works with those people who are normally withdrawn and incapable of such communication!

6. *Don't provide any evaluations or opinions regarding the person's expressed attitudes or feelings.* This takes a lot of practice and self-discipline, but don't you sit in judgment!

Don't criticize! But, then, don't sympathize, either! Just try to be objective. Any opinions from you at all (either negative *or* positive) may cause the person to regret having opened up to you. The doors of communication will then close again.

But why not show sympathy, you might wonder? Even sympathy is a type of judgment. It tells a person that you've stopped listening and started to evaluate—before they've had a chance to completely present their case. It casts doubts on your objectivity, even if it *is* a bias in their favor. After all, if you're not completely fair *this* time, how can they have confidence that *next* time, *after they've opened up their soul to you,* they won't find themselves on the opposite side of your good graces? That's emotionally frightening, and will prevent a person from revealing on a deeper level, where you could have even greater influence.

7. *Let the other person reveal himself or herself to you at their own pace.* Don't push. If they seem to wander illogically in their conversation, let them! Don't try to direct any thoughts back to where *you* believe they should go. Just try to understand the main gist of the conversation from moment to moment. If they want to stop talking altogether, fine! Be willing to accept that. Don't try to dig for information the person may not yet be ready to reveal. By providing a non-threatening atmosphere in which they can express themselves *at will*, without fear of criticism or judgment, you'll soon be *sought out* by *them* "just to talk." This kind of patient listening is rare indeed, and they'll soon recognize that being with you satisfies a life-long thirst they've always had. It is doubtful whether anyone else will ever be able to give them such a deep sense of being *understood*.

The more understanding you provide for the one you want, the greater influence you'll have with that person. In addition, that person will become more strongly attached to you. The importance of reflective listening as a tool in your arsenal to win love cannot be emphasized too much. It is perhaps *the most essential tactic of all* to include in your overall strategy for successful romance. Practice and use it!

LOVE TACTIC #32 Avoid Being Critical

Although certain practices are essential for success in love, there are others that must be *avoided*. What's one of the biggest no-no's? *Giving criticism!* Although people invariably try to justify this action by claiming that they're merely trying to help the person "improve," the sad fact is that it very rarely has this effect.

Experience has shown that the only predictable result of criticism is the weakening of trust in human relationships. It's true that occasionally a person will take a critical, judgmental remark to heart and make some beneficial changes because of it. But it *still* makes them less willing to open up and be vulnerable to the person who criticized them. And if you're trying to win someone's love, this loss of trust is completely self-defeating. If they really need to have their faults pointed out, fine. *Let someone else do it!*

Consider your own feelings in this matter. Think about the last time someone offered you some so-called "constructive criticism." How did you react? (Be honest, now!) Not too well, right? Even if the critical observations were true, they were undoubtedly painful! What happened afterwards? Did the experience increase your feelings of *fondness* for that particular individual? Of course not! Even those who don't show their hurt still *feel* it! *And they won't be anxious to repeat such an experience,* so it will only be a matter of time before they'll start avoiding their critic. *Don't let that critic be you!*

You can often be critical without even realizing it. Although you may guard against it in most cases by first asking yourself, "How would I feel if someone were to say this to me?," there are still a few subtle types of criticism that we may not even be aware of:

1. *Using the word "why?."* If you want to really set someone on edge, try using this single-word interrogative about five times in a row in casual conversation. But do so at your own risk! If you end up in the hospital, we'll have to assume that you underestimated the maddening effect this little word can have on people. But don't say we didn't warn you! The word "why?" creates an automatic defensive response. By using it, we unintentionally demand others to justify themselves to us, or to justify their perceptions of things.

   Think about it. Perhaps this is the reason why it becomes so exasperating to an adult when a little child asks "why a thing is so." The adult gives his best answer and the child asks "why?" again. Although the adult may not be aware of the cause of his irritation, it's because the adult's whole value system is put on trial each time that word is used. In some ingenious way that the adult is helpless to understand, the child has made himself the judge, and the grown-up the defendant. That can be exasperating!

   If you sincerely want to understand someone's reasons for doing a certain thing, or believing a certain way, without any intention of passing judgment on their motives, try to soften your interrogation so that it shows you simply want *to understand*, not *judge*. Generally, you can do this by simply saying, "Could you help me to understand some of the reasons why it seems to be so?," or "Could you help me to understand why that course of action seems best?" This will show your willingness to assume good faith on the other person's part, and a desire to understand rather than to judge. And this will be very effective in helping the one you want to feel less criticized.

2. *Giving advice.* As the proverb goes, "Don't give advice. Wise men don't need it, and fools won't heed it." But, you must be informed, they *will* resent it! All advice says, in effect, "You know what you oughta do? Well, let me tell you . . . !" It implies that the person being given the advice is unable to figure out for himself what direction his own life should take. That can be extremely demeaning.

    But people will try to trick you into it, nonetheless! They'll come to you asking, "What should I do?" *But don't fall for that old trick!* What they really need is someone who will reflectively listen to them. If you don't believe this, just think about how many people in your own life have already ignored your advice—even when they came begging for it in the first place! This is because people *already know, in the back of their minds, what they should do.* Knowing *what* to do has never been the problem. They're just experiencing some sort of subconscious conflict about actually *doing it! That's* the problem! And your telling them again what they should do, when they don't really *want to do it,* only enhances their sense of *conflict, guilt,* and consequently, *resentment towards you* for tormenting them further. So save your breath—and advice. What people really want when they ask for advice is *a listening ear.*

3. *Criticizing while claiming you don't intend to.* This can be the worst form of criticism. It feigns friendship, but proves disloyalty. It goes like this, "I don't mean this to be critical, *but. . . ."* It's hard to avoid a tightening of your stomach muscles when you hear these words addressed to you. Often the person doing the criticizing thinks that qualifying his statements in this way somehow makes them less offensive. Wrong! We often feel *more* hurt by someone who pretends to be a friend and then criticizes us, than by a proven enemy who has been openly hostile all along.

    These few subtle forms of criticism that you may unintentionally use in your relationship are by no means exhaustive. They are just examples of the many ways in which you may unwittingly be critical. Be constantly on guard against using them.

The moral of the story? If you want to be loved, *don't criticize!* The less you indulge in criticism, the easier it will be for others, including the one you want, to love you. It's a good tactic to remember. *Avoid being critical!*

LOVE TACTIC #33 Express Genuine Admiration And Praise

Over the years, marital therapists have learned some great lessons about behavior through their first-hand observations of human relationships. For example, it has been noticed that *the intensity of love feelings one person will experience towards another in a relationship occurs in direct proportion to how important and worthwhile they believe they are in the eyes of that other person.* In other words, the more important a person feels that he or she really is to you, the stronger and deeper will be their reciprocated feelings of love, dependence, and attachment for you.

THE VALUE OF FEELING VALUABLE

There is a good reason for this. One of the most important human needs, next to feeling unconditional acceptance, is to feel valuable. Don't *you* need to feel important? Don't *you* need to feel that you have real worth? Well, others have these needs, too! People not only need to feel accepted in spite of their faults, but also need to be recognized and appreciated *for their positive qualities.*

This type of emotional need can only be satisfied by others. Effectual praise and recognition *cannot be self-administered!* Self-praise is just too shallow. No matter how much a person tells himself "I'm great!," another voice deep inside echoes back "Who do you think you're kidding? Can't you see that your credibility is flawed—your motive is suspect?"

Objectivity is the first requirement of a credible judgment. And deep down, all of us intuitively realize that it is impossible to be emotionally detached and objective about ourselves. Just as nature has decreed that no human being can ever actually see their own face, so has it denied them the ability to objectively view their own character. *We need others!* It is only through others that we can comprehend our own existence. Like blind men, we depend on others to describe to us what we "look" like and to tell us if we possess any beauty. If there is anything admirable or praiseworthy in our character, it must first be described to us by someone else willing to be our "eyes." *We just can't trust our own judgment in such matters.*

Now how does all this tie in with winning the one you want? In this way: The one you want is a human being with a need for admiration and praise, which *they are helpless to satisfy alone. If you are aware of this and make a conscious effort to satisfy their hunger in this respect, they will develop a deeper dependence on you.*

THE REASSURANCE OF BEING REASSURED

Most people are literally starving for such emotional reassurance! That's why your effective expressions of genuine admiration for another person will go far in cultivating that person's love for you. In spite of popular teachings to the contrary, the truth is that *the opinions of others always have more effect on what we think of ourselves than all the self-affirmation we can muster.* Patting yourself on the back all day long will not make you even one fraction as confident as a single pat from another person who says, "Well done, John!" or "Good job, Sue!" Thus, recognition of our positive virtues *must* come from another person if it is really going to mean anything to us. By expressing genuine admiration and praise to the one you want, you'll be meeting an emotional need that they are incapable of satisfying for themselves.

ADMIRING ADMIRINGLY

Now that you're aware of the importance of admiring the one you want, you need to be aware of three points in order to express genuine admiration effectively.

First, you must convince the person you're admiring that your appraisal of them has real merit. You must persuade them that your judgments are cautiously discerning and, therefore, accurate—that you are not praising out of a mere sense of loyalty to them. How can you do this? *Spend time getting to know the person. Listen first, in order to understand.*

Earlier in the book you read about the use of flattery to enhance your likability. Although flattery can (and *should be*) sincere, it may be regarded as a *premature evaluation* (perhaps rightly so). Herein lies its true deficiency. Both the giver *and* receiver usually recognize such compliments as superficial observations made *in passing*. Flattery alone, therefore, won't satisfy a person's deeper emotional needs. How can you penetrate more deeply? *By investing the time to really understand the person.* If you really want to get your praise across, you must first spend time getting to know the *real* person behind the mask through reflective, non-judgmental listening.

Second, after you've made the effort to get to know the real person, consciously note that person's good qualities. Every person has traits worthy of admiration. *Every* coin has two sides, and even negative behavior is usually just a distorted form of some positive, but frustrated, trait. A marital counselor once pointed out to the wife of an alcoholic husband that his sneakiness was just a twisted form of creativity, while his tendency to indulge in self-pity was evidence of undeveloped compassionate abilities. She then admitted that his job did require much creativity. And she had always noticed how quick he was to show concern for others. Everyone has good qualities waiting to be discovered. Find them!

Third, having found those qualities worthy of admiration, tell the person what you have discovered and observed! Praise their virtues. Tell them how much you benefit from their association. This will show the person how important they are to you. By so doing, you'll encourage that person to be willing to depend on you for a greater sense of worth. And this, in turn, will draw you one step closer to a fulfilling love relationship!

LOVE TACTIC #34 Supply Sympathy

Everyone needs some sympathy from time to time. Sometimes people try to act like they're above this need, but they usually turn out to be the ones who need it most. By giving sympathy to the one you want in a time of need, you can greatly relieve their emotional burdens and strengthen the bonds of attachment that they feel for you. It is a law of human nature that people gravitate towards those who help them through emotionally-difficult times.

Since sympathy is a form of personal judgment (although admittedly a positive one), the same rules apply for its use as for giving meaningful praise: *Do not give it prematurely!* The Bible says, "He that answereth a matter before he heareth it, it is folly and shame unto him." Spend time trying to understand how the person really feels before offering words of intended comfort. Otherwise, the sympathy you give will appear shallow and won't have the lasting impact you want it to. Sympathy should only be given *after* a deeper level of mutual understanding has been reached through empathic, non-judgmental listening. What does that mean? *Listen reflectively first!* Then, after your sincere effort to try to *understand them without judging them* has been firmly impressed in the person's mind, offer your sympathy. He or she will be much more receptive to, and appreciative of, the sympathy you offer.

The word *sympathy* means "together in feeling." People need to know they're not alone in how they think and feel about things. All you need to express, therefore, is something along the lines of, "You know, I don't blame you a bit for feeling that way. I'd feel the same way under similar circumstances."

Easy, isn't it? Whether it's fear, anger, or just plain emotional pain that is burdening the one you want, reassuring
statements of sympathy will work wonders in restoring them
to a happier state of mind. This can't help but make the person more emotionally dependent on you. Don't neglect opportunities to supply sympathy. It's another key to winning
the one you want!

9

Shaking Their Confidence

---

*Principle: The more insecure a person feels
about where he or she stands with you,
the more vulnerable they will be to
your romantic advances, and the more
intensely they will desire you.*

People can never fully appreciate someone's love if they are allowed to take that love for granted. There must be some ongoing apprehension that the love so freely given could be lost at any time. Always remember this: *While people disrespect that which they have in the palm of their hand, and are attracted to that which they can't get, they become absolutely frantic with desire over that which they already possess but are in danger of losing!*

Therefore, in order to successfully stir up someone's romantic passions for you, you must create some uncertainty on their part regarding your feelings for them. It becomes necessary to create a gnawing fear in their mind that, in spite of your general appearances of devotion, you're still constantly on the verge of changing your mind about them. They must be led to believe that, at any given moment, they could lose you forever! When you do this, you've set the stage for romantic passion and love to really blossom.

Insecurity is the mother of infatuation. Doubt is the key to unleashing another's potential for experiencing romantic passion towards you. In the midst of the garden of love and friendship that you cultivate and freely offer to someone, plant some seeds of doubt. This will keep them wondering if they really *do* have you, after all. The following tactics suggest ways of doing this.

LOVE TACTIC #35 Use Silence

What do you think would happen if you unexpectedly stopped talking to your partner in the middle of a date and suddenly became very silent during the remainder of your time together? This simple technique can be one of your most subtle and effective ways to tune up a relationship. It will get the person you're with to start doubting their influence over you and wondering if they're losing your interest. It will motivate them to become more attentive to your needs to try and maintain their hold on you. But this tactic requires fixed determination. Why? Because the unsettling effects of silence on a relationship can disturb *you* as much as *them!* The temptation for you to say something and get the conversation going again can become almost overpowering. Wise is that person, however, who exercises self-discipline and resists this temptation, allowing the power of *silence* to work its disquieting miracle on the one they want. Those who learn to use this tactic appropriately will ultimately reap rich rewards from such an exercise of patience.

The nice thing about silence is that it leaves *everything* to the imagination of the one you're with. And when you're dealing with people's insecurities and self-doubts, imagination is always your best tool. *Telling* a person that they're in danger of losing you is not nearly as effective as *letting them wonder!*

One young man, whose story is not at all uncommon, used this tactic with the girl he later married. He appropriately made use of it at a time in the relationship when she had begun to take his constant attention and tokens of affection for granted. Her appreciation of him was at a low, so one night when they were out together he turned on the silent treatment as he was driving her home. This was quite a change from his normal, outgoing self and, of course, she noticed it right away. As they drove along and the silence continued to build, the quiet completely undid her, emotionally, and shook her confidence. (That's what you have to do: *Shake their confidence!*) For the first time in a long while she felt him slipping away, got quite humbled by it, and asked him to pull the car over. When he did so, she told him with tears in her eyes that she had a feeling she was losing him, and asked if anything was wrong. She was ready to start making amends!

This sort of reaction is not unusual, folks! It worked for one aspiring lover, and it will work for you, as well. Use this tactic to your advantage. Even if the one you want doesn't outwardly appear to be concerned about losing you, you can rest assured that this technique *will* cause them to secretly worry and wonder if such is the case.

Another hopeful suitor, motivated by the above example, reported his attempts to use this tactic on a pretty and popular girl who had previously acted somewhat aloof towards him. Even though she finally agreed to go out with him, she didn't show too much enthusiasm. In fact, all evening long she acted kind of bored and didn't contribute much to the conversation at all. It was as though she were thinking, "Ho-hum, let's get this over with. I can't wait until he takes me home and drops me off!"

Meanwhile, her date forced himself to exude enthusiasm by remaining very talkative and friendly throughout the evening. He acted as though he wasn't even aware of her mood. It was obvious that she felt she had him wrapped around her finger, so her behavior remained like that of a spoiled child.

Then, about ten minutes before dropping her off, he decided to stop paying attention to her. He stopped smiling at her. He even stopped looking at her. And he *completely* stopped talking to her. He just kept his hands on the steering wheel and his eyes on the road ahead. It seemed as though his thoughts were suddenly a million miles away, and he acted totally preoccupied and aloof!

He knew *exactly* what he was doing, but she had *no idea!* This was certainly a stark contrast to the attentiveness he had exhibited throughout the earlier part of the evening. After a few minutes the thought obviously crossed her mind that, uh-oh, she might have offended him. (In fact, that's exactly what she had been unconsciously trying to do—brush him off without making herself appear like the bad guy.)

Even though she had previously wanted to discourage him, she certainly didn't want him to be *mad* at her. So for the first time that night, *she* tried to pick up the conversation herself, while he responded with short, preoccupied answers, as though it was too late. He was polite, but that's about it. He made no efforts to really enliven the conversation, as he had previously. In short, he was *giving her back some of what she had been giving him all evening, and it was beginning to unnerve her.*

His original plan was to just drop her off without any further conversation at all. He wanted to leave her wondering what had happened—wondering if he had suddenly stopped liking her, or what! But then the most amazing thing occurred! She absolutely came *alive* in her efforts to revitalize his interest in her. She not only began making enthusiastic efforts to get him reinvolved in the conversation, but started throwing all sorts of compliments his way and commenting about what a wonderful evening she had been having. And then, when he still didn't seem to be won over, she went to great efforts to convince him to come in for a while. Being condescendingly nice, he went in for a few minutes. However, he didn't stay long.

This is an instance where, with a very simple method, the tables of desire were quickly turned. The girl's attitude toward her date from then on was much more appreciative and respectful.

Don't be afraid to use the silent treatment when appropriate. If you don't pull in your welcome mat once in a while, eventually you'll be completely taken for granted. And that would be *fatal* to your hopes of inducing romantic interest in you by the one you want!

So, occasionally turn on the silence! Yes, let it get good and loud! If you have the courage to let the one you want go home at night with the echo of silence still ringing in his or her ears, it will, ironically, stimulate passion and stoke their fires of emotional desire for you!

LOVE TACTIC #36 Drop 'Em Cold!

Nothing—absolutely nothing—can turn a person's disinterested, uncaring attitude around and make them burn with feverish romantic desire for you like being dumped! Marital therapists have long been aware of this typical, predictable reaction in human relationships. A person's apathetic feelings will immediately turn into passionate longing when they realize that a possession which had previously been taken for granted is in danger of being permanently lost.

A classic illustration of this can be seen in the relationship between Rhett Butler and Scarlet O'Hara in the classic motion picture, *Gone With The Wind*. Throughout almost the entire story, Rhett Butler remains selflessly devoted to Scarlet in his attempts to win her love. Only when he walks out on her in the end with his famous line, "Frankly, my dear, I don't give a damn," does she finally realize that she can't live without him!

This type of situation is more true to life than most people realize. Take a similar incident that happened to a young college woman. A particular young man, whom she had no interest in whatsoever, took a deep romantic interest in her and began courting her with a passion. He showered her with phone calls, drop-in visits, and other bits of attention. She says that, at the time, she just felt kind of annoyed and irritated by it all. In spite of the many brush-offs she gave him, though, he persistently hung in there and showed he cared.

Finally, she got her wish—or, at least, what she *thought* was her wish. He gave up on her! He abruptly stopped coming around and calling. And would you like to guess what happened? "I actually started missing him!," she admitted.

You see, unknown to either of them, the attention and selfless love he had been showing her all along had been developing a subconscious bond of affection inside her for him. It was *only when he dropped her,* however, that she recognized her own hidden feelings and became aware of the fondness that she had developed.

This type of reaction is not uncommon. *It is the rule!* In many cases, though, this unforeseen advantage to the suitor is lost. Why? Because the "dumper" never returns to the "dumpee" to pick up where they left off. By making such a second effort, the dumper would find a much more responsive and appreciative dumpee eagerly waiting for a second chance!

Every salesman knows that, in order to get a customer to buy, there has to ultimately be some sort of urgency element in the decision-making process. Never a message of "whenever you get around to it, it'll be here waiting for you . . ." but "if you don't buy today, you may not have the opportunity tomorrow!" The psychology of selling is especially operative in romance, because the exchange of vows made in marriage is the most important sales transaction a human being can ever make! The message you have to convey is "It's now or never!," and you have to reinforce the impact of this message by letting the person experience a little bit of what life without you can be like.

One girl who had been taken for granted for years by her boyfriend's non-committal attitude finally informed him that she was taking a job offer in another city and moving away. Not thinking that she had the intestinal fortitude to ever leave him, he asked her how she could even think of doing such a thing. She responded, "I love you, Monty, but I can do fine without you." Well, that completely undid him, just as he deserved to be undone, and he proposed one week later! But if she hadn't shown her ability to drop him cold and go her own merry way, they'd probably still be hanging out there in limbo to this very day! Just remember—most addictions are not realized until the source is cut off. If you never let the one you want experience the pain of withdrawal by losing you for a while, they may never become fully aware of how hooked they really are on you!

Wouldn't it be a shame to spend your entire life always being taken for granted by the one you want? Often, one good demonstration of emotional muscle-flexing is all that is needed! Just showing how painful life can be without you will forever keep the one you want appreciative and respectful of you.

Some people claim that such tactics are exploitive and immoral. Not true! Yes, whenever you strive to enhance your own situation through the impairment of someone else's, you are being exploitive. But when you attempt to improve someone else's position, *along with* your own, then that is *good business!* (This is generally referred to as the "Win/Win Philosophy.") Ideally, *both* parties in any human exchange or transaction should benefit, and that is certainly the aim of this book.

Knowing this, be bold and courageous! After you've been persistently selfless in a relationship, don't be afraid to drop 'em cold. Let them know what it's like to live without you for a while! Then magnanimously return to the one you want and give them another chance. You'll be surprised at the effectiveness of this tactic!

LOVE TACTIC #37 Create Competition

Would you like to stir up the latent passions of the person you want and get them to actually *crave* your affections? Then create a challenge for them! Give your special someone something to be jealous of. Don't let them think they're the only show in town! Have many friends of the opposite sex. Go out and spend time with them socially. Don't be afraid to flirt a little, either! It will absolutely amaze you how much a little rivalry can stir up a person's hot-blooded romantic desires for you!

One young man had been dating a girl somewhat casually for four years, until he found out that she had begun dating someone else. Upon hearing this he immediately began to experience passionate feelings that he didn't think he was capable of. Both his appreciation and affection for her were elevated to new heights!

Similarly, the one you want is a latent bomb of passionate feelings just waiting to be set off. All you have to do is light the fuse! Ann Landers once defined love as "friendship that has caught fire!" If this is so, then the key to love (once you have established a good, solid friendship) is to somehow take that particular relationship and create some combustion!

The tactic of creating competition, of course, is as old as romance itself. In fact, browsing through a used bookstore recently, someone came across a copy of *Ovid's Love Books*, written almost two thousand years ago for the citizens of ancient Rome. (It seems that *nobody*, not even the originators of romantic love themselves, has ever been immune to the frustrations brought on by affairs of the heart!) The reader was surprised to find that as long ago as *that*, Ovid was strongly recommending the use of a *rival* to stir up the reciprocated affections of one you want!

But in spite of people's awareness of how well this technique works, many refrain from ever using it! Their reasoning is simple: They've narrowed down their interests to one person, so why waste their time on others? There are two very good reasons to keep yourself in circulation, though. First, if you're to be fully appreciated by the one you want, *then they have to feel lucky to get you.* It is therefore necessary to create the illusion that your affections could be lost *to someone else.* As the one you want becomes convinced of this possibility, their appreciation of you will soar. Second, as you interact with others (dating, just being friends, flirting, or whatever), your own emotional need for companionship will be somewhat satisfied. This will make you a stronger and more self-confident person in other aspects of your life, *including your relationship with the one you want!* This, in turn, will help you to

radiate a spirit of confidence and independence, further challenging your special person to new emotional heights. So
don't become a hermit! Play the field! *It's good for you and for
the one you want!*

LOVE TACTIC #38 Break A Date!

Although breaking a date with someone runs the risk of getting them angry at you, this is precisely why it can be such an
effective tool in winning their love! It shows a person that
you're not intimidated by their opinion of you or what you
do. It's a subtle way of reasserting yourself in a relationship at
a time when the other person is beginning to think that he or
she is "in control!" By breaking a date, you cause the person
to doubt their ability to dominate you, which will in turn fan
the flames of their romantic passion for you. Remember: People crave the unobtainable. They *most* desire to conquer that
which appears invincible. Breaking a date can re-establish the
challenge for the one you want and create heightened interest
and longing for you!

One young man found this out only after a number of fail-
ures with previous romances. He stated that he always tried
to be open and honest with the ones he wanted, but found
that his openness only drove them away. Time after time they
would lose interest in him, always leaving him shortly after he
confessed to them how much he cared.

Finally, his instincts began to tell him that it was this very
openness that was destroying all these good possibilities. So
he tried a new tactic. Instead of confessing devotion when a
new relationship began to warm up, he called the girl on the
phone and broke an approaching date.

Afterwards, he says, he spent the night worrying (even *cry-
ing!*), thinking he had perhaps blown one of the best things to
ever come along in his life. *But he didn't blow it!* Where others
had deserted him at this particular stage in previous relationships, this girl fell madly in love with him! You see, he had

maintained the challenge of romance for her and she had responded accordingly! So don't be afraid to use this tactic. It will work for you, too!

10

Keeping Them Interested and Hoping

Principle: In order to keep a person's romantic passions stirred up, they must be given some spark of hope that you could still reciprocate their feelings. Without this hope, interest in you will ultimately die.

Romantic infatuation is a delicately-balanced human response. It thrives on *uncertainty.* On the one hand, too much self-confidence in a person will kill excitement. On the other hand, no confidence at all *will starve it to death.* So while keeping the one you want from any certainty that you're hooked on them, you must still provide them with some glimmers of hope *that you might become so!* How do you do this? Read on.

LOVE TACTIC #39   Resume Contact (After Temporary Lull In The Relationship)

Once you have established some basis for the other person to think you are losing interest, you are ready to proceed. Surprise the person by once again calling them up on the telephone. Start dropping by to see them anew. Most importantly, start asking them to *go* places with you and *do* things together again!

Have you realized yet that part of the overall strategy of this book is to keep the one you want somewhat confused and off balance? You don't want the person to know quite what to expect from you next! This requires that your interest *appear to shift from hot to cold, and then back to hot again!* (You may have heard of this before as *"blowing hot and cold."* Well, it works like *magic* in mesmerizing the one you want!) Any seasoned lover knows the importance of varying the approach while developing a relationship. This type of unpredictability is as essential to romantic survival as *changing colors at will* is to the continued existence of a chameleon.

As a general rule, people are more prone to respond when given a second chance to maintain their affiliation with you. This is because they are much more motivated! They won't always be able to fully appreciate the blessing of your affection until they've experienced the void that comes in its absence. Thus, when an opportunity to regain it comes along, there will be much greater appreciation and passionate desire. So after letting the one you want stew in the prospects of having lost you for a while, resume contact and *give them that second chance!*

Just because the going gets tough does not mean that the relationship is over. It's not over until you quit. So don't be afraid to take a tough stand from time to time, to scold if necessary, or even to break off contact with the one you want. *But don't fail to resume contact and pick up where you left off after the smoke clears. You'll be surprised at how positive the results will be!*

LOVE TACTIC #40 Send Mementos

After you've created some uncertainty on the part of the one you want about your feelings toward them, send a small memento of your affection to revive their hopes. Whether by a short note or a small gift, any message you communicate should remain vague and non-committal. Keep actual words in any written communications at a minimum. The very fact that you are taking the time to send *anything at all* intrinsically gets the message across that you care.

A word of caution, though. Beware that you do not send mementos too early in a relationship, or at a time when the other person is already over-confident as to your feelings for them. If this happens, such additional evidence of your love will only be taken for granted. The very person you hope to win may end up disrespecting (and even despising) you! Yet this is a common mistake of naive lovers. Don't feed an already oversized ego! Remember that passion thrives on insecurity! Before you make a person's day by sending them a token of your affection, make sure that they are experiencing intense doubts about your fondness.

LOVE TACTIC #41 Awaken Physical Attraction

The exhilarating experience of "falling in love" is unquestionably a sex-linked phenomenon. Whether you're consciously aware of it or not, the mainspring of all romantic activities is the instinctive sexual drive of the human species. Its constancy and strength is what keeps husbands and wives and, consequently, families together in the first place. Without it, few people would ever be sufficiently motivated to commit their entire lives to another individual in such an exclusive arrangement as that of marriage.

For this reason, then, it is futile to expect to win someone's heart completely and fully without being able to stir up some physical desire for you. And that, dear friend, is why *kissing* was invented! Serving as much to stir up passions as to gratify them, kissing is an invaluable tool for helping to bond couples emotionally and prepare them for marriage. It provides a subtle incentive for increased physical closeness. It is a tool (much like fire) with a similar potential for good or bad, through proper or improper use. If used wisely, the fires that are awakened can motivate people to make the commitments necessary for permanent relationships. But if allowed to burn out of control, they can destroy any possible hope of permanency in a relationship.

"That's just fine," you might say, "if you can get the person to kiss you in the first place! But how do you get over *that* hurdle?"

No problem. The underlying philosophy of *Love Tactics* is that a person must *act*, not *react*, in order to succeed at romance. So when the other person shows no inclination to initiate affection, *you* be the aggressive one. It doesn't matter if you're male or female, as long as you've already established a firm foundation of friendship and respect before making your move. It doesn't matter who takes the initiative, as long as *somebody* takes this step. In fact, marriage counselors often find that their male clients actually *want* the woman to be the aggressive one in the relationship!

Make sure the one you want is comfortable with your physical closeness by engaging in non-sexual touching first. Everyone desires the warmth of physical affection and human touch. Sometimes, however, the person you have designs on may be uncomfortable either expressing *or* receiving physical affection. Why? Often it is because the person is just not accustomed to close physical contact. In such cases, you may gradually "condition" a person to being touched by you. How? By proceeding very patiently. Begin by touching the person you are with in a non-sexual way, briefly, and from time to time whenever you are engaged in conversation. In time, gradually increase the duration of contact, as well as the frequency. A person's back, shoulders, and arms are generally safe, nonthreatening parts of the body that can be touched with little risk of a traumatic emotional response.

Eventually, however, you must move on to the real thing. When you finally *do* kiss, don't act like you intend to "test the waters" first, one toe at a time, carefully watching every reaction. Just go for it! Act as though you've made an independent decision about what you want to do. Act as if it's irrelevant to you whether the person has any desire to kiss you back or not. Make it seem almost as though it's just a game to you—a lark or a challenge—and that it's no big deal if the person's not interested in kissing you back. (By the way, the first kisses are probably better being short and sweet. A long, passionate, suffocated kiss right away may result in a short, unpassionate, suffocated relationship! Make it a *fun* thing, rather than a *serious* event.)

What happens when the one you want does *not*, in fact, want to kiss you back? That's no big problem either! It's o.k.! Don't let it throw you! Haven't you ever heard of *stealing a kiss!? Trying* to kiss the person is *part of the process of warming them up and instilling the desire!*

Remember—success in romance (or in any other project in life, for that matter) is dependent on your willingness to *act* independently of other people's opinions, and not merely to *react. Love Tactics* is not merely a system of guidelines to analyze people and figure out whether their whim of the moment is to *like* you or not. Rather, it's an active system of principles to help you *win their love,* whether they like you at first or not!

What happens if the one you want turns away from your initial kissing overtures? Just carry on with normal conversation as if nothing happened. Ignore any rebuff as if it's no big deal. Later, in the quiet hours of reflective contemplation *after* the date, the seeds of desire will begin to grow. The one you want will begin to fantasize about what it might have been like *if* . . . and the next time they will!

When your kiss is returned, kiss with enthusiasm, but not for *too* long! *You* be the one to end the kiss. Don't make it too long. It's better to leave the person hungering for more, rather than bored by too much! Why? Because if you continue so long that the other person feels the need to terminate the experience, you'll diminish your influence in the future. Remember: *You* be the one to initiate and *you* be the one to say when enough is enough. Keep control of the relationship. It will drive the one you want wild!

As to the more passionate physical intimacies commonly sought and indulged in, you'll find them contrary to the focus of this book. It is strongly advised to avoid them altogether until you are married! This may not be what you want to hear, but past experience only confirms the wisdom of this counsel. Historically speaking, people in nations with strict codes of morality and chastity have been happier. The more intimate physical privileges traditionally reserved for marriage are, in fact, the very *enticements* of marriage itself! To engage in them prematurely and, in effect, *give away your bargaining chips for nothing,* only cheapens your own worth to the other person. It can destroy any chances of developing a real sense of commitment in the relationship. *Somebody* is going to be used, and there will not be enough respect to cultivate the full and complete romantic love necessary to the happiness of both parties. Frequently, however, couples indulge in such mutual exploitation without realizing the damage they are doing to the relationship.

And make no mistake about it—the ultimate goal of *Love Tactics* all along has been to convince the one you want that they should marry you! The most rewarding love of all is that which exists *in the institution of marriage!* But if you surrender your body and soul in full measure to another person prematurely, without requiring them to marry you first, you will unwittingly sabotage your efforts to attain this objective!

Sure, premarital sex is highly prevalent in today's modern society. But look around you! Isn't *unfulfilled love* just as prevalent? You see, it's not that premarital sex is harmful because it's disapproved. Rather, it's disapproved because it's harmful! It spells the difference between a temporary relationship and a *lasting* one.

We will, however, stand by our recommendation to use kissing to enhance a relationship, remembering to maintain control at all times. Prudently engaged in, kissing will help you to secure a commitment and win lasting love from the one you want!

11

Confronting Diplomatically

---

*Principle: When the one you want feels completely
understood and accepted by you,
their ability to resist loving you will go
right out the window. They'll find themselves
falling in love with you in spite of all contrary
logic and their best efforts to resist.*

One of the most challenging obstacles you will ever encounter
in your pursuit of the one you want is their tentative assessment that you can't handle the truth. They'll figure it would
hurt you too much to tell you straight and simple, for example, that they don't want you (other than just as a friend). So,
trying to be kind, they'll look for some other way out of the
relationship without disclosing their real reasons why.

However,, if you allow them to get away with this avoidance of confronting you with the truth, *that* will actually be
the fatal factor and coup de grace to the relationship. You
must prove to the one you want that you not only can face the
truth, even if it means your being rejected by them, but that
you can accept it without being shattered. The more crucial
issue here is not really one of their not *loving* you, as their not
believing you love *them*.

If they feel that deep down you don't really understand their doubts and fears, then they must conclude you really don't know and accept *them*, as the person they truly are. If they believe that you would be crushed and embittered towards them if you knew how they really felt about you, then they must conclude that your love for them is shallow and *conditional*, based upon some fantasy version of the person you merely *think* they are.

Miraculously, though, as soon as you can demonstrate to them that you can not only sense their true feelings, but *accept them*, even in the face of your own personal rejection, their very doubts and previous objections will become unimportant to them. When being faced with the realization that, "My goodness! Here's a person who *really* cares about me, in spite of myself!," their other reasons for hesitation towards you will pale in comparison with the prospect of being truly loved for *who they are!* And when a person feels truly understood, accepted, and, yes, loved, somehow all the other prior concerns which seemed so important to them before suddenly don't mean so much anymore. They'll find themselves falling in love with you, in spite of all the reasons they can think of why they shouldn't. In the final analysis, after all, love is truly a language of the emotions—not logic!

LOVE TACTIC #42 Confront Resistant Behavior

As you attempt to develop a relationship with someone you want, quite often they will begin to experience doubts about what they are getting into. They will begin to have a number of extremely logical, personally convincing, *secret* reasons why the relationship is all wrong and will, in their hesitation to get in any deeper, begin to show distinct signs of resistant behavior towards you. This will manifest itself in symptoms of moody behavior, guarded and unresponsive communication, disrespect towards you, and, finally, outright avoidance of you.

Such behavior needs to be confronted. If the feelings underlying this type of behavior remain buried, they will ultimately destroy the relationship altogether. But through unselfish and caring confrontation on your part, such resistance may be defused and rendered powerless. Such a method is outlined below. Think of it as a way to show you CARE: Confront, Ask, Reassure, and Empathize.

Confront the person's uncooperative behavior. "Maybe I'm mistaken, but I sense that something's wrong . . ." One of the most exhilarating experiences a person can have in life is the feeling of being understood. We don't want to have to *tell* others when we are feeling distraught. We want them to sense it on their own. *We want them to read our minds!* As one disgusted wife tried to explain to her imperceptive husband as she was in the process of divorcing him, what every spouse wants in a companion is "someone who can read them like a book!"

What people don't often realize is that they subconsciously give clues as to what they're thinking by the way they act. Being sensitive to such unspoken acts and confronting the one you want will go a long way in satisfying their need for understanding. This, in turn, will eliminate emotional obstacles to their becoming committed to—and loving—you.

Ask for a confirmation or denial of your observations. "Am I reading you right? *Is* something actually bothering you? . . ." By informing the one you want of the message that their behavior communicates to you, and then asking for a validation of your interpretation, they will be impelled to come to grips with the actual meaning they intended to convey. "Hmm . . . I *have* been acting rather cold and distant . . . Now, what exactly have I meant by this? What have I been trying to communicate here?"

The important thing is to make the person consciously aware of their own motives in their actions toward you. Indeed, they have already been intimating something all along which, subconsciously, they would like to be able to say to you. All you're doing is calling their bluff and inviting them to say what's on their minds. In order to do that, though, they have to first decide exactly what *is* on their minds, and if it's worth mentioning or not. That requires a little bit of thinking on their part. By inviting them to put their feelings into words, you are forcing them to *crystalize their feelings into defined terms that can be dealt with.*

People often behave in a certain way without really knowing why. Until *they* know exactly how they feel, *you won't be able to help them.* The first step in changing someone's attitude is to get them to recognize *for themselves* what that attitude is.

At this point it doesn't really matter if they're ready to come clean and openly admit their newly-discovered feelings or not. The mere realization that you have *already* been listening to them *with your heart,* and are willing to listen more, will go a long way in stripping the one you want of their power of resistance. In the long run, logic cannot withstand the force of emotion. The sense of fulfillment that the one you want will experience from feeling understood and accepted by you will ultimately override any hesitation they may have about surrendering their heart to you.

Don't push the person for more details than he or she is ready to give. *You don't need to.* You've already brought them to a crossroads in the relationship—to a point where they must make a choice between honesty and repentance. Both are good, and either will strengthen the relationship. Either they must admit what's been troubling them to explain their behavior, or they must *change* their behavior to be consistent with their denial that anything is wrong!

Reassure the person of your intention to merely understand (not judge) on the basis of what is admitted, especially if there seems to be a little hesitancy for them to express their feelings. ". . . Because I'm willing to just listen, if you're willing to talk. I just care how you feel . . ." The biggest reason for breakdowns in communication is the fear of being judged. Human experience has shown that our honest feelings will not always be accepted by others without comment or criticism. Some encouragement from you will be necessary to assure the other person that they will not be thought less of because of their personal fears or concerns.

Finally, **empathize.** Be understanding. Once the person does start to open up a little bit, don't blow it! Just listen, like you promised you would. Don't criticize. Don't try to change the person's mind or show how their reasoning is wrong. If you do, you'll regret it, because it will be a long, *long* time before the person will ever open up to you again.

Let the person proceed at his or her own pace. If you're not yet too competent at reflective listening, just nod your head and say "Mm-hmm . . . Yes, go on . . ." But *don't* pronounce judgment on what is being said.

The acid test, of course, is when the one you want admits to having doubts about the relationship. Don't panic when he or she states that the two of you are not right for each other! Remain calm, no matter how much of a personal rejection their words may become! *You are still going to win out!*

The only way to defuse such sentiments, though, is to allow the person to get them out in the open and have you be *completely accepting of them.* Showing that you disagree with these feelings will only reinforce them in the individual. (Of course this doesn't seem to make sense, but it's really how it works!) Be totally accepting at the time of the discussion, but reinitiate contact with the individual several days later, without warning, and show your intentions to maintain this friendship—even without romance. *You may rest assured that romance will come along in due time.*

Your willingness to let the one you want open up to you at a pace comfortable to them, coupled with your obvious sensitivity that something was bothering them in the first place, will encourage them to rely more and more upon you. This method of understanding is one of the finest ways to communicate love and overcome any obstacles that may be blocking romantic progress with the one you want!!

12

Demonstrating Commitment

---

*Principle: The more convinced a person
is of his or her personal importance to you,
the more intense will be their feelings
of love for you.*

After all is said and done, the ever-present question being
asked by both participants in a relationship is, "How important am I to you, *really?*" All other questions are mere off-
shoots of this one. The more valued each feels to the other,
the greater will be the feelings of love they will have in return
for their partner. The following tactics discuss ways of demon-
strating how much you value the one you want.

LOVE TACTIC #43 Hang In There!

Occasionally, after all is said and done, it will appear that the
one you want is completely unmoved by your efforts to win
them over. *But don't be fooled by such deceptive appearances!* This
seeming ability to resist you indefinitely is simply *nature's way
of shaking out those pursuers who are less sincere—and less committed.* The challenge you face is to prove through your endurance that your love is *true.*

In your frustration, though, you may find yourself asking, "What am I doing wrong . . . ?" If you've faithfully done your best to apply the tactics in this book, the answer is, "Nothing." You are on the right track. You just need to keep using *Love Tactics* a bit longer, and more skillfully, as you learn from your mistakes and improve with practice. In due time, reciprocation will come.

You're allowed to make mistakes, too, by the way! It's o.k. if your voice shakes occasionally, or if you fall flat on your face every now and then! You're only human, and people will still love you in spite of these things—maybe even *because* of them. Just keep getting back up and trying again. The only permanent mistake you can really make is to *quit*.

If you have had a handful of dates with a particular person and still feel like you're not making any progress towards winning them over, don't be discouraged! Not too long ago an article was written by Dr. Joyce Brothers that should encourage every hopeful but frustrated lover. Commenting on a survey of married couples, she disclosed that *over half* of the women said they didn't feel that they were in love with their husbands-to-be until *after at least twenty dates!* In other words, you really can *grow* to love someone. Human experience indicates, similarly, that men are likely to grow to love those women who patiently continue to interact with them.

THE VALLEY OF THE SHADOW OF APATHY

How well can you hang in there? This depends on your ability to persevere *even when you occasionally lose all feelings of desire.* In other words, expect that there will come a point when all the excitement you first felt for this special person will temporarily dissipate. You may find yourself thinking, "Wow! Before, all the pain seemed worth it. But now I feel like I don't even care anymore! Before, it seemed like the one I wanted was worth *any* price. But now I'm not even sure I'd want them if they came begging!"

But "this, too, shall pass." You're actually closer than ever to your goal. *Now* is the time when your true ability to love will be tried. This is because love, in its ultimate form, is a commitment of pure will power—with no gratification attached.

This doesn't mean that you don't deserve happiness and emotional fulfillment anymore. You *do*, and it will still happen. But first you must walk through *the valley of the shadow of apathy* to claim your prize! Be forewarned that this experience is inevitable in any developing, worthwhile relationship.

Is it reasonable to ask you to hang in there forever, with no desire or hope of gratification ever again? Of course not! But the truth is: *If you hang in there for a while, in spite of your temporary loss of interest, your feelings of desire will eventually return.*

If you're truly committed to endure to the end, there is no heart that you won't be able to win over. To quote a well-known maxim, "The race is not to the swift, not the battle to the strong, but to him that endureth to the end."

Sometimes it may seem awfully frustrating and you may not know all the answers. But rest assured, *there are answers. There are solutions. There is a way.* It's just a matter of persisting until you find out what that way is. *You can do it!!*

LOVE TACTIC #44 Say "I Love You"

Although earlier in this book we stated that you shouldn't wear your heart on your sleeve, there does come a time in a relationship when it is wise to say "I love you." But that time comes only after you have consistently proven your love—not with *words*, but with *actions*. Words are cheap, and people know it. Remember: "What you do screams so loudly in my ears, I can't hear a single word you say!"

The main thing to remember in expressing your love is that *people run from commitments.* If someone suspects by your words that what you are really saying is, "I want a commitment from you," it may inadvertently drive them away. Use the words "I love you," but try to do it in the context and intonation of, "It doesn't matter to me whether you return my affections or not. My desire for your happiness stands, regardless!" The degree to which the one you want actually believes this will determine your success in winning their love. Your words must somehow convey the message that your love is an unconditional commitment to their happiness, with no strings attached. It mustn't come across as an attempt to back them into a corner where they'll feel obligated to say "I love you" in return. People will *not* allow themselves to be trapped this way! Expect much, gain little. Expect little, gain much!

Remember, though, that these three little words can lose their potency if your actions contradict them. Think of the words "I love you" as the bullet, and your actions as the gunpowder. If you put a bullet in your musket without having packed in a good supply of gunpowder first, then upon firing your weapon your bullet will fall harmlessly to the ground. On the other hand, if you forget to load the bullet, even though you have packed in a good supply of gunpowder, your firearm will not accomplish its purpose, either.

When America first came into being, the nation's position was a fragile one. American armies didn't have the expertise or strength of the Royal British Forces. Nor did America possess the financial resources of England. Colonel William Prescott, who led the American troops at the Battle of Bunker Hill, realized the precariousness of his untrained army's position against much better armed forces. As they observed the enemy advancing up the hill, he advised them, "Don't shoot until you see the whites of their eyes!" He knew they might not get a second chance, so every shot had to count.

Likewise, when you're trying to win the one you want, realize that there will only be so many opportunities to effectively say, "I love you." But don't say it too soon, or the words may seem as though they have no real force behind them.

Patiently prove your love first. Keep watching the one you want advance steadily "up the hill to the slaughter." Then, when you can see "the whites of their eyes" and sense that the words will have the proper impact, *fire away!* If you imagine that you've got only one shot and have to make it count, you'll intuitively be more capable of choosing the right moment to say, "I love you!"

13
Removing Final Barriers

Principle: By backing off from a relationship that you have been aggressively pursuing for some time, the other person will automatically let down his or her emotional guard and, thus, become more vulnerable to your renewed advances in the future.

Often, when a person continues to resist you, it is because they think you haven't gotten the message yet. Oh, yes, perhaps they realize that you are aware of their *declared intentions* to stay uninvolved and uncommitted to you. But they just think you haven't yet realized how *serious* they are about it.

Backing off from the relationship for awhile can take care of all that! The real issue at this point is to convince them that you really understand that they mean business in their determination not to get involved with you. This is the only effective way to convince them that you understand, and in the final analysis you're going to have to demonstrate your ability to communicate with them if you're ever going to win their heart over. If you can succeed at communication, it is only a matter of time until you can turn the tables on their rejecting attitude towards you. Once you've shown your ability to understand, you'll be on much more sure ground to stage your comeback.

LOVE TACTIC #45 Strategically Withdraw

Among the famous legends of ancient Greece is the story of the Trojan Horse. For ten long, frustrating years the Greeks had assaulted the city of Troy in an unsuccessful attempt to win back their beautiful queen, Helen. The walls of the city were impenetrable, though, and the Greeks found it impossible to get inside. Direct confrontation appeared hopeless. Finally, in desperation, they resorted to a much more *subtle (and effective!)* strategy.

The Greeks built a large wooden horse, hiding some of their soldiers inside. They left it standing outside the walls of Troy. Then the rest of the army boarded their ships and sailed away, making it appear as though they had abandoned their cause and given up.

When the Trojans first found the horse, they were fascinated by it. *No longer feeling threatened by a direct confrontation with the Greek army, the Trojans let down their guard.* They not only opened their gates, but *brought the monumental horse into the heart of the city,* as a memento of their unexpected "victory."

That night, while the Trojans slept, the Greek soldiers inside the horse disembarked and again opened the gates from the inside—this time to their waiting comrades who had sailed back in the dark of night. The city was destroyed and Helen was saved. Strategic withdrawal had accomplished in a single day what ten years of direct encounter had failed to achieve!

Likewise, after aggressively pursuing the one you want and finding the stony walls around their heart to be unyielding to your love, employ the Trojan Horse strategy! Make a strategic withdrawal! The sense of relief that most people will experience when they can finally let down their emotional guard will be great, and upon a fresh new encounter with you, they will not be willing—or able—to resist.

The great lesson of the Trojan Horse is that those things that cannot be accomplished by pure force can often be accomplished through strategy. Love is not something that can be forced. But by using strategies of persuasion based on behavioral psychology principles, it *can* be induced!

LOVE TACTIC #46 Enjoy Being With The One You Want!

After all is said and done, love ends where it begins. In a word: *Commitment!* The desired object of love is to have someone who is truly committed to you and to your happiness, but it begins with your commitment *to them!*

The reason why so many love affairs don't work out is because neither person in the relationship was ever truly committed to the other person's unconditional acceptance and happiness. Each one expected the *other* to demonstrate commitment *first*. But when someone becomes clearly aware that you are truly committed to love them *unconditionally*, it is guaranteed that he or she will then love you back. As Ralph Waldo Emerson once said, "Love, and you shall be loved."

When you have accomplished all that you've set out to do and finally win the one you want, enjoy! Nothing material can compare with being happily in love, so take the time to stop and appreciate what you have! Realize that love is worth more than all the treasures on earth. So be aware of this fact, and quietly give thanks to divine providence. Good luck, and enjoy being with the one you want!

Conclusion

There you have it! The formula of the ages! Practice these principles and they will enrich your life immeasurably. It is the authors' fondest wish that you may have a happier life through their application.

The overall philosophy of *Love Tactics* can best be summed up in the poetic words of Emmet Fox:

*Love**

There is no difficulty that enough love
will not conquer; no disease that enough
love will not heal; no door that enough
love will not open; no gulf that enough
love will not bridge; no wall that enough
love will not throw down; no sin that
enough love will not redeem.

It makes no difference how deeply seated
may be the trouble, how hopeless the outlook,
how muddled the tangle, how great the mistake; a sufficient realization of love will
dissolve it all. If only you could love
enough you would be the happiest and most
powerful being in the world.

*Dr. Emmet Fox, "Love Card" (DeVorss & Co.: Marina Del Rey, California). Reprinted with permission by Blanche Wolhorn and Hedda Lark.

Good luck with *Love Tactics!* As you apply these principles in your life, you'll become increasingly convinced—as we are—of their effectiveness in winning the one you want.

If you have any questions or a particular problem that you'd like some additional guidance on, please feel free to write to us in care of the publisher. We'd be happy to hear from you! Please share your successes with us, as well! The greatest reward any author can receive is knowing how much their book has helped someone!

Index